PRAYER FOR COLLEGES,

A

PREMIUM ESSAY,

WRITTEN FOR

"THE SOCIETY FOR THE PROMOTION OF COLLEGIATE AND THEOLOGICAL EDUCATION AT THE WEST."

BY

W. S. TYLER,

PROFESSOR OF GREEK IN AMHERST COLLEGE.

NEW YORK:
PUBLISHED BY THE SOCIETY, 80 WALL STREET.
1859.

PRAYER FOR COLLEGES,

A

PREMIUM ESSAY,

WRITTEN FOR

"THE SOCIETY FOR THE PROMOTION OF COLLEGIATE AND THEOLOGICAL EDUCATION AT THE WEST."

W. S. TYLER,

PROFESSOR OF GREEK IN AMHERST COLLEGE.

NEW YORK:

PUBLISHED BY THE SOCIETY, 80 WALL STREET.

1859.

[FROM THE NINTH REPORT OF THE SOCIETY—1852.]

PREMIUM OFFERED.

A benevolent individual, deeply impressed with the importance of multiplying the number of educated and evangelical ministers of the Gospel, in order to meet the pressing and growing wants of our country and of the world, has placed at the disposal of the Society for the promotion of Collegiate and Theological Education at the West, the sum of one hundred and fifty dollars, to be given to the author of the best Essay on "PRAYER FOR COLLEGES."

The writer is expected to set forth the *importance* of the subject, especially as relates to the conversion of young men in a course of education and the consequent increase of candidates for the sacred ministry. Also the *encouragements* derived not only from the divinely appointed relations of prayer to the conversion of men but also from the signal answers to prayer for this specific object furnished by numerous revivals of religion in Colleges. Then, by way of *inference*, the *obligations of Instructors* to labor unceasingly for the conversion and sanctification of those under their training, and of pious young men in Colleges to co-operate in this work—together with the obligations of Boards of Trust, to whom the church in an important sense, commits the sacred interests of Christian education.

Committee of Award.—Rev. Prof. Ralph Emerson, D. D., of Andover Theological Seminary; Rev. E. N. Kirk, Boston, Mass., and Rev. L. F. Dimmick, D. D., Newburyport, Mass.

PREMIUM AWARDED.

Newburyport, June 28th, 1854.

The Committee for awarding the prize ($150) "To the author of the best Essay on Prayer for Colleges," have received and examined thirty-two manuscripts. Many of the Essays are written with ability, and several appear well worthy of publication. The one best adapted, in the judgment of the Committee, to accomplish the purposes of the donor, is found to have been written by Prof. W. S. Tyler of Amherst College.

An earlier decision has been prevented by the absence of one member of the Committee for a considerable period from the country, and by other unavoidable circumstances.

In behalf of the Committee,
RALPH EMERSON *Chairman.*

'Prayer and Pains can accomplish any thing."

ELLIOTT.

"I never prayed sincerely and earnestly for any thing, but at some time, in some shape—probably the last I should have devised—it came."

JUDSON.

"The man who would show to common minds the connection between colleges and the interests of the church, would be a benefactor to his species."

DWIGHT.

"The Schools of the Prophets are there; is it not a more extensive benefit to sweeten the fountain than to purify a particular stream?"

WESLEY

PREFACE.

THE subject of this Essay divides itself into two parts —*prayer* in general, and prayer for *colleges.* The first three chapters are devoted to the former; the latter fills the remaining chapters.

It may perhaps be thought that the discussion of the subject of prayer in general is too extended, if not quite superfluous. But in the opinion of the writer, the weak point of the church in our day lies just here; and it would be of little avail to present colleges, or any other *object* of prayer, in all its magnitude and importance, unless Christians in general can be brought up to a higher appreciation of the *efficacy* of prayer, and to a more vigorous appliance of it as the most potent of Heaven's appointed *means* for the salvation of men.

Others may deem some apology necessary for the extent and miscellaneousness of the second part of the discussion. Possibly some of the topics may appear too secular to be introduced at all into a treatise on Prayer for Colleges. In answer to this, the author would only plead the fact, that so much is written and said in our day to mislead and prejudice the public mind in reference to colleges, and his conviction, which he shares in common with Dr. Dwight, that Christians in the common walks of life are still far from a right understanding of the real character, merits and relations of colleges to the church and the community. In this view, he has aimed to furnish a kind of *Manual* or *Epitome* of the services which the college has rendered, not only to the cause of learning and religion, but also to human progress and human happiness.

If the Essay has any merit, it consists in the simplicity, directness and earnestness with which it labors to show to "common minds," 1st, the duty and the power of believing prayer, and the peculiar necessity of more faith and prayer in our day; 2dly, the indissoluble connection between colleges and all the great interests of the church, the country and mankind ; and 3dly, the sacred obligations, primarily of the officers and students, and those immediately concerned ; but secondarily, of all who have an interest at the throne of grace, to bring this great power to bear on this most important point.

At the same time, it is hoped that the *educated* Christian men of the country, and Christian ministers especially, will find not a little in this Essay to "stir up their pure minds by way of remembrance ;" and the writer is deeply sensible that its power to do good will depend very much on the manner in which it is received, sustained and enforced by those whose experience attests, and whose life illustrates the value of a college education. For himself, he claims to have written only what he believes with all his heart, and what he knows from his own observation and experience. The beloved College with which it has been his happiness to be connected, either as a pupil or as a teacher, for nearly twenty-five years, was founded in faith and prayer ; and those numerous and powerful revivals of religion, which have so conspicuously marked its whole history, have followed almost visibly in the train of the special prayers of those who have been connected with it, or concerned for it. If there is any thing in this Essay that is adapted to be useful, it is the fruit of prayer; and if it should prove, in any measure, subservient to the cause of learning and religion, it will be through the divine blessing, in answer to the prayers of the many devoted men whose hearts are already enlisted in this sacred cause.

W. S. Tyler.

Amherst, *November* 20*th*, 1854.

PRAYER FOR COLLEGES.

CHAPTER I.

The Duty of Prayer—Recognized by all forms of Religion, and sometimes practised even by Infidels—Homer, Socrates, Thomas Paine—Results from the nature of Man, from his circumstances, and from his relations to God—Pericles and Demosthenes—Taught by the Word and the Spirit of God—The dictate of common Humanity—The Offspring and Expression of Christian love—Martyn.

PRAYER, in its most comprehensive signification, is "the offering up of our desires to God." In a more restricted sense, it is asking the favor of God for ourselves, or for others. It is not only an unspeakable privilege, but an imperative duty, imposed on every human being by the law of his existence, by the necessary relations which subsist between him as a dependent, needy creature, and God as his infinite Creator, bountiful Benefactor, and compassionate Father. It is a duty which he owes, not only to himself and to his Maker, but also to his fellow-men, imposed upon him not merely by the instincts and intuitions of his nature, but by the dictates of reason and the law of universal benevolence. It is made still more imperative on *Christians* by the revealed will and direct command of God—being placed in their hands as a sacred trust and a mighty engine of power, which they are as sacredly bound to employ for its proper purposes, as any other trust whether of talent, or property, or influence.

Prayer is recognized as a duty and a privilege by every form of religion that has ever existed in any part of the world. The most degraded Hottentot prays to his Fetische, though it be no better than a snake or a stick of wood. The Hindoo, of whatever rank or caste, bows in adoration before his ugly idol, confesses his sins, and deprecates the displeasure of a *thing* which cannot harm him—implores the favor of a thing which is impotent to help its worshippers. The polished Greeks and Romans, with purer taste though with little better reason, offered their supplications with their sacrifices in the presence of those sculptured forms of beauty and grandeur, which embodied their highest conceptions of human excellence, deified and exalted to the skies. Some heathen poets and philosophers have set forth no unworthy sentiments respecting prayer. Homer represents Prayers as Jove's daughters, lame, wrinkled and slant-eyed, that is, feeble and deformed in themselves, but mighty as messengers and mediators between earth and heaven; and as an illustration of the power of prayer, we see in the Iliad the wasting pestilence fall thick and terrible as the arrows of a god on the Grecian host, in answer to the supplications of the injured priest of Apollo, and at the intercession of the same priest, when righted and appeased, the shafts of the destroyer cease to rain upon the people. Socrates rebuked those who did not look to God in prayer for guidance and assistance, as setting the weakness and ignorance of men above the wisdom and power of God; and God was, in his view, better pleased with the spiritual homage of the truly pious, than with the most costly sacrifices of the wicked. Infidels pray, despite their infidelity, when they are suddenly brought into circumstances of trial and danger. Thomas Paine, when in peril of shipwreck, called loudly on God to have mercy on him; and men who denied the divine existence, have been so oppressed by a felt want of divine teaching, that they have poured out their supplications into the blank and drear vacuity by which they were surrounded.

No age, no nation, no religion has ever existed without prayer; and it may well be doubted, whether any individual has ever lived to mature age, who has not, at some time or other, in some way or other, offered prayer. The very universality of its prevalence proves it to be the dictate of nature. The foundation for prayer is laid in the very nature of things, in the relations that exist between God and his creatures. It results necessarily from God's greatness and goodness, and man's weakness and wants.

Man's own moral and spiritual nature bids him pray—pray for himself, and also for others. He is but a child, and he must needs run to his Father for sympathy, support and assistance. He is ignorant of what none but God can teach him. He is weak, and

God alone can strengthen him. He is guilty, and God alone can forgive him. He is miserable, and God only can comfort him. He has his peculiar individual wants and trials, which he would fain unbosom to none but a sympathizing, all wise and all merciful Father. He has also interests and necessities in common with his friends, and neighbors and fellow-men, which their united wisdom and power are utterly insufficient to provide for. Mankind are, in fact, but one great *family* of *children*—gathered on the footstool of the Most High, sitting, as it were, continually at his feet; and surely it were most unnatural, it were passing strange, if they had no questions to propose to their Father in Heaven, no counsel to seek at his lips, no favor to ask at his hands, no delight in looking up into his face, and reading there the expressions of his complacency and parental love. The impulse to prayer is, like filial affection, almost an instinct in the breast of man; the duty of prayer, like filial duty, is perceived, as it were, by *intuition*.

And the circumstances in which we are placed, are eminently adapted to call this instinct and intuition into active exercise. For the voice of external nature unites with that of our own souls in exhorting us to prayer. The heavens over our heads bid us look up to One who is higher than we; and the stars in the silent night whisper of One who made us, and who, though far above us, yet bends an ear to our requests. The earth beneath our feet invites us to adore the goodness that has overspread its surface with fruits and flowers and every pleasant thing; and yet the same earth bids us tremble before the awful power and justice that has made it, within, a portentous magazine of heaving forces and ever-living fires. The elements around us, whether in tranquillity or in commotion, teach us our dependence, our impotence, our nothingness before God, and call on us, now in gentle tones, and now in a voice of thunder, to praise him who scatters the gifts of his beneficence in the rain and the sunshine ; to pray to him who rides upon the whirlwind and directs the storm. We are not only children, but children surrounded by elements which we cannot control—dwelling in a world of wonders, which we cannot comprehend—encompassed by a universe, whose grandeur and vastness are quite overpowering to our feeble faculties ; and we must be strangely perverse and depraved, if we do not cry to our Father for instruction and for help. If we listen to the teachings of nature, there is no lesson which she will teach us in more commanding or more inviting tones, than the duty of prayer. The world in which we live is a temple built expressly for worship, and man is the only conscious intelligent worshipper.

Nor is the duty, the necessity, of prayer less obvious, when we direct our attention to human society and human affairs in their manifold relations. There too we soon find ourselves looking up to heights which we cannot scale—trembling on the verge of depths which we cannot fathom—moving amid elements and forces which we can neither comprehend nor control. A few steps in any direction carry us beyond the boundary which separates the known from the unknown, the practicable from the impracticable, the human from the Divine. There is no subject so simple that we can know it fully, no enterprise so easy that we can accomplish it independently. Man is bound by a thousand links to his fellow-man; and the entire chain with all its links is suspended on the will of God. How blind then must that man be who does not pray—pray for himself, and also for others!

The future is an unfathomable abyss—who can penetrate its unknown depths? No man can foresee the issue of a single day, or secure with certainty the desired result of the smallest undertaking. Shall not every man then pray to Him who sees the end from the beginning, and who holds the future, not less than the present, in his all comprehensive grasp?

The human heart also is an abyss—who can fathom it? Who can know all the depths and windings of his own heart? Who can trace or imagine the countless mazes of the many hearts, whose interests and affections are bound up with his own—whose secret purposes and intentions may most deeply concern him? The human will is an element of incalculable tendencies and forces—who can control it in its stormy rage? who descry its secret workings, and gathering energies in its seeming tranquillity? And a community, a nation, a world of such hearts and wills, or even an assemblage of them, for whatever purpose gathered—who can sway them at his sovereign pleasure, and guide them with absolute certainty in right channels and to good results? None but He who can command the winds of heaven, and they shall obey him.

That man then is a fool who enters upon any undertaking, involving any important interest, whether his own exclusively, or of a more general nature, without prayer to the Being who holds the hearts and wills of individuals, communities and nations—as he does the winds and waves, and all the elements of nature—in the hollow of his hand. So sensible of this were the greatest statesmen and orators of heathen antiquity—such for instance as Pericles and Demosthenes—that they often commenced and concluded their speeches with a prayer. The very *language* of all nations reflects a dim consciousness of the duty and necessity of prayer: for what are all the salutations and other forms of address, especially in the glowing East, but disguised forms of prayer—prayer for that richest blessing, *peace*, on our friends and neighbors; and what are all the *hails* and *farewells*, the *adieus* and *good-byes*, even of the colder occidental nations, but the language of prayer—though too often uttered by thoughtless lips and with unconscious hearts.

Now, if such be the necessity, such the obvious duty of prayer in worldly enterprises and temporal interests, how are both the necessity and the duty magnified, when the soul's immortal welfare is at stake! Who can make his own salvation sure—who secure the salvation of his friends and neighbors, and fellow-citizens and fellow-men? Who can foresee the issues and provide for the destinies of eternity? It is high as heaven; what canst thou do? deeper than hell;

what canst thou know ?—the measure thereof is longer than the earth, and broader than the sea. No sooner does a sinner become truly anxious for his soul, than he begins to pray, though he never prayed before. Never was there a Christian, who watched for souls as one that must give account—who felt that he was intrusted with the care of immortal beings whose weal or woe for eternity was suspended on his influence—never was there such a Christian that did not give himself to prayer.

Just in proportion as one appreciates the value and estimates the hazard of eternal interests, just in the same proportion will he be instant in prayer. The teachings of nature, the promptings of intuition, the yearnings of his own soul, though he had no other instruction, would constrain him to call on God, for wisdom, which no earthly friend can impart, for help, which no created arm can give.

But we are not shut up to the light of nature to teach us the duty of prayer. We have the more sure word of revelation. God speaks from *above* as well as from within and around us, and calls us to prayer. It is his will as communicated to us from the *lively oracles,* that in all things, by prayer and supplication with thanksgiving, we should make our requests known to God ; that we should cast all our cares, however trifling, upon him who careth for us, and commend all our interests, however precious, like our souls at death, into his hands who waiteth to receive them ; that we should pray for our fellow-men of all classes and conditions, whether more or less closely connected with us, but more earnestly and importunately as they are more related or intrusted to us, and as their station is higher and their influence more widely extended.

The duty of prayer is inculcated in the Scriptures, not only by precept, but by example. The patriarchs wrestled with God in prayer, and prevailed. The prophets leaned on prayer as the sceptre of their power. The apostles and primitive Christians were strong in and by prayer. Jesus not only gave his disciples a formula of daily prayer, but set them an example of habitual prayerfulness. When about to perform some especial duty, or encounter some peculiar trial, he would sometimes spend the whole night in prayer. Throughout the Bible, prayer is not only the breath of spiritual life, but the staff of spiritual strength, the weapon of spiritual warfare, the engine of miraculous power, the channel of temporal and spiritual blessings, the medium of all heavenly gifts and divine communications.

Nor is it in the Bible only that God—the Christian's God—teaches men to pray. He writes the lesson in their hearts by his Holy Spirit ; and then it is said of every new born soul, as of Saul of Tarsus : Behold, he prayeth. Prayer is pre-eminently characteristic of him that is born of the Spirit. The heathen pray, but prayer with them is a blind instinct ; with the Christian, it is an intelligent principle. With them, it is a dictate of nature ; with him, it is the inspiration of the Holy Spirit. The unregenerate man may pray ; but before regeneration prayer is a reluctant duty, or a felt necessity ; after conversion, it is a delightful privilege, a supreme pleasure, a ruling passion. Then he delights in it, as a way of access to God, and communion with him. Then he relies on it, as a channel for the communication of all needed good things, of all temporal and spiritual gifts. Then he uses it diligently and joyfully, as a means of his own growth in grace and progressive sanctification. Then also he learns to pray, not merely for himself, but also for others—for his friends, his acquaintances, his fellow-citizens, and his fellow-men, for the kingdom of God and the cause of the Redeemer. He prays for the sanctification of his Christian brethren, even as for his own. He bears impenitent sinners on the arms of prayer and faith to a pardoning and life-giving Saviour, as men brought their sick and their dead to the same sympathizing and almighty Friend, when he tabernacled in the flesh. He rests on prayer as his own solace and support under affliction, leans on it as a sure prop and pillar of the Church in the day of her adversity, and applies it as the only lever which can lift up this fallen world once more into the light of God's countenance.

Take prayer from the Bible, and you take away not only the essence of the devotional books, but the substance and the life of the doctrinal and historical portions of the Scriptures ; and vital Christianity is gone—there is only the semblance of religion left. Take away prayer from the human soul, and you have removed its best solace, its only sure support. Take away prayer from the world, and you shut out from it the light of Heaven, cut it loose from the throne of God, and leave it to wander in perpetual night, a cold and barren, "a forsaken and fatherless world." Take away prayer from the Christian, and you have robbed him of the pilgrim's staff—from the Christian minister, and you have taken from him the shepherd's crook,—from the Christian family, and you have closed against them the door of access to their Father's house.

Prayer for our fellow-men is the dictate of common humanity. The irreligious man—the skeptic even—cannot look upon a suffering friend or neighbor without a spontaneous desire for his relief, cannot bend over the couch of a dying fellow-mortal without an outgoing wish for his recovery. Such a wish gushes forth yet more freely from the Christian's heart, but in his breast it is no longer mere desire, it is transformed into prayer, and he pours it out in a tide of glowing emotions, and, if circumstances allow, of fervid words too, into the ear of a prayer-hearing God. It were inhuman, as well as unchristian, for him not to do so. If he does not do it, how dwelleth the love of man—not now to speak of love to God—in his bosom ? And is it less inhuman for him to look upon a fellow-sinner, who is vexed with the cruel malady of sin, and ready to die a spiritual and eternal death, and offer no prayer for his salvation ? When a word, a breath may be all that is needful to save him from the untold agonies of the death that never dies, shall that word, that breath be withheld ?

What would you think of the humanity, to say nothing of the Christianity, of the man who, in the days of our Saviour's incarnation, when he went through the cities and villages of Palestine healing all manner of sickness and all manner of diseases among the people, would not lend a helping hand or raise an encouraging voice even, to bring the blind and the lame, the palsied and the possessed, the dying and the dead, into his sacred and life-giving presence? And yet *thou* art the man, if thou dost habitually pass by thy unconverted friends and neighbors, and not lift up one silent prayer for their conversion. Nay, thou wouldst charge thyself with even greater inhumanity than his, were thine eyes opened to discern spiritual things as they are, inasmuch as the health and life of the soul are infinitely more precious than those of the body, and Jesus is *ever* present, and ever waiting to be gracious to afflicted souls.

If we saw an uninterrupted succession of our fellow-men defiling in chains before our eyes, and then dropping, one after another, into a dungeon of unknown depth and hopeless gloom, and knew that petitions—earnest and importunate petitions alone—could break their chains and secure their deliverance, what heart so obdurate as not to join in such petitions? And where is our compassion, where our fellow-feeling for our fellow-men—to say nothing here of sympathy with God and Jesus Christ—if we do not offer up earnest and unceasing prayers for a whole race of human beings, the greater part of whom are still the bondslaves of Satan, and are falling, one every second, into the dungeon of unending despair! Oh that the eyes of men—of Christian men—might be opened to see, and their hearts to feel, the *inhumanity* with which they are chargeable, in withholding that manner and that measure of prayer which is the indispensable means of a world's salvation! And would that it might be given them fully to understand, what a priceless opportunity and what inexhaustible resources for world-wide charity and divine philanthropy are put into their hands when they are permitted to pray for a spiritually diseased and dying world!

Prayer for others is the natural and almost necessary expression of Christian love. Love to God, love to Christ, love to the souls for whom Christ died, all demand from every Christian a life of prayer.

Love to God is essentially filial love corresponding to that parental affection—the fulness of a father's with the tenderness of a mother's love—which the universal Parent bears towards all his children. Or rather it should be a *more* than filial love answering to that *more* than parental affection which the Christian's God and Father cherishes towards those who are not only the creatures of his power, but the children of his grace, and who are the objects at once of his infinite benevolence and of his divine complacency. Now nothing is more characteristic of affectionate parents, than a willingness to give their children any thing that is really for their good—nor is any thing more characteristic of dutiful children, than the delightful confidence with which they ask their parents for any thing and every thing of which they feel the need. Behold then our Heavenly Father standing with his hands ever full of the richest gifts, his heart ever longing to lavish them on his children, and his lips ever saying to them: Ask what I shall give thee! And say what could be more unfilial to such a Father, than to ask no favors at his hands? what more grateful to his parental heart, or more becoming the winning attitude in which he stands, than that we should be as ready and delighted to ask, as he is to give? Especially, when we have been undutiful and even prodigal sons, and our Father stands waiting to forgive our wanderings and to rejoice over our return, shall we not return to him with earnest, and if need be, importunate prayers, that he will restore us not only to his favor but also to his image? And having been thus forgiven and restored by his matchless grace, so long as there remains an ingrate and a rebel among all the family of man—the proper family of God on earth—shall we not pour forth our intercessions in behalf of that wayward child, and never cease to pray that God's name may be hallowed, and his kingdom come, and his will be done, till he is adored on earth as in heaven!

Behold also Christ—who sustains towards his disciples the relation at once of a master and elder brother, and who deserves in return a half-filial, half-fraternal love from them—behold him standing at the door of human hearts and knocking for admission, his locks wet with the dew of the morning, his feet bedewed with precious blood, one hand laden with blessings which he has purchased for them at infinite expense, and the other pointing to heaven, where it is his desire that they should be for ever with him. And tell me, can Christians who bear his name and bear his likeness, behold this moving spectacle and not pray day and night, that he may see of the travail of his soul and be satisfied; that he may have the heathen for his inheritance, and the uttermost parts of the earth for a possession? Will they not spend the breath of their mouth for that which cost him the life-blood of his heart? Can the children of God be willing that their heavenly Father should always be disowned by the greater part of his family? Can the disciples of Christ be content, that their Lord and Master should be always despised and rejected of men? "It were hell to me," says Martyn, "if he were to be always thus dishonored." Will Christians suffer the souls which Christ hath bought with his own blood, to be lost, if they can hinder it by their prayers? Nay, if they have any proper sympathy with Christ, if they have aught of the spirit of apostles, martyrs, and missionaries of whatever age, the very thought of such a continual waste of his precious blood, and such perpetual dishonor to his holy name, would so fill them with sadness that their burdened souls could find relief only by unbosoming their sorrows in unceasing prayer to their heavenly Father and their divine Redeemer.

CHAPTER II.

The Power of Prayer—The Incidental Benefits of Prayer in its Natural Effect on the Soul—But these pre-suppose a Belief in its Direct Efficacy—The Westminster Assembly—Prayer is Asking, that we may Receive—The Instincts of the Lower Animals unerring—Much more the Soul's Instinctive Belief, that God will hear Prayer—Various ways in which Divine Veracity is pledged to do so—How this Pledge has been fulfilled in Sacred History—Prayer always a Ruling Power in the History of the Church and the World—An Elementary Force in the Constitution and Course of Nature—A Fixed Fact and an Established Law in the Economy of Providence and Grace—Its power not impaired, but destined to be most prevalent in the Last Days of the Church.

In the foregoing chapter, we have endeavored to show that prayer is a duty both of natural and revealed religion ; being, as it were, an instinct of the soul, and a dictate of nature and of common humanity as well as of Christian piety.

We wish now to proceed one step further and demonstrate, that it is a *great spiritual force in the world*, and a *mighty controlling power in the divine government.* And in so saying we refer not to its incidental effects in quickening, purifying, and elevating the soul of man. Such an influence it *does* indeed exert in many ways ; and it is an influence, whose power and importance can hardly be over-estimated. Prayer, in its very nature, directs the thoughts towards the highest, greatest, and purest objects, and thus tends to elevate, enlarge and purify the soul. Prayer fixes the affections and desires on the noblest and best ends, and by the very act of expressing those desires (according to a well-known law of the mind), increases them. It fastens the eye of the mind in a steadfast gaze on the image and glory of God, till that image is daguerreotyped, as it were, on the soul ; nay, till the soul itself is "changed into the same image, from glory to glory, as by the Spirit of the Lord." Prayer brings the mind into such a state of desire and yet of dependence, of patient waiting and yet of earnest longing, as prepares it to prize, enjoy and profit by the blessing, when, in answer to prayer, it is bestowed. Intercessory prayer for our Christian brethren and our fellow-men, strengthens our love for them, cultivates charity and patience in our feelings towards them, and prepares us to relieve their wants, and comfort their sorrows. Most of all, prayer brings man into the felt presence of his Maker, and in that presence, if any where, the sinner will learn to abhor himself and repent in dust and ashes—there, if any where, the Christian will cleanse himself from all filthiness of the flesh and the spirit, perfecting holiness in the fear of the Lord.

When one *already believes* in its *direct* efficacy, these incidental benefits are all so many auxiliary and powerful inducements to "be *instant* in prayer." And it is a striking illustration of the divine benevolence, which should call forth devout gratitude, that in this, as in so many other (we might perhaps say *all* other) divine arrangements, the greater good involves the less, and the path of duty leads to unsought, unexpected, incidental blessings.

But these incidental effects presuppose a direct efficacy as the basis on which they rest. Remove this, and the entire superstructure falls to the ground. Without a sincere and heartfelt faith in the efficacy of prayer to procure actual blessings from God—without a deep conviction that God hears us when we pray, and really grants us the good things we need *because we ask for them*—prayer does *not* bring us into the presence of God,—does *not* take hold of his outstretched hand, and therefore does not lift us up to his throne,—does not bring down his promised Spirit, and therefore does not hallow our bodies as his temple, or purify our hearts as his inner sanctuary,—does not fasten the desires on all that is brightest and best in heaven as a proper object of expectation and desire, which we can secure by asking, and therefore does not either add intensity to such expectations and desires, or open any practicable way for their realization. Just so far as our faith fails to lay hold on the promised blessings as *really* to be *obtained* by *asking*, just so far prayer will fail to prepare our hearts to receive them ; and just in proportion as we discredit the direct efficacy of prayer, just in the same proportion we impair its incidental benefits.

Indeed prayer, without any expectation or belief that God will hear or answer it, is *not* prayer ; it wants the essential element of prayer, and deserves not the name. It may be called meditation ; it may be considered in some sense as communion with God ; it may even be regarded as a species of worship ; but it resembles more the dreamy, misty, transcendental contemplation of the Boodhist, than the real personal access of the Christian (with his petition as it were in hand, and his mouth full of arguments) into the presence of a heavenly Father, and a sympathizing, incarnate Redeemer. Prayer without a petition addressed to some one who is accustomed to hear and to grant such petitions, and that with some expectation or hope that it may be granted, is an absurdity, a contradiction in terms. Nay, is not the very name and form and attitude of prayer a mockery, if it neither has, nor can have, nor is expected to have, any real and proper influence in obtaining blessings at the hand of God?

Imagine (if the idea is not too preposterous even for the imagination to frame a conception of it) Abraham pleading for Sodom, not with any expectation of saving the devoted city, not with any hope of exerting the slightest influence on the mind and will of Jehovah, but simply for the sake of the reflex influence of the interview on his own character, or the personal pleasure and profit of talking with the King of kings! Conceive (if it is possible to conceive of a thing so absurd and ridiculous) of a man getting up a petition to some fellow-man—a sovereign or some other civil ruler—not with any expectation that it will be granted, not with any belief that such petitions ever are granted, or have any influence with the ruler, but simply for the sake of the purifying and elevating effect which the process of getting up the petition will exert on the mind of the petitioner, or as a mere contrivance for awakening distinct thoughts and lively emotions touching the sovereign, and cheating himself into the belief, or the fancy, that he has thus made his way into the royal presence! None but a maniac could ever thus delude himself in mere worldly relations. But let him have a petition to present for an object on which his heart is set, let him come into the actual presence of a great and good prince, and plead his cause with all the eloquence of truth and earnestness, and see the face of his sovereign, beaming with wisdom and complacency on him, and hear his voice granting the request, or if not granting it, expressing his sympathy and approbation in language that is as cheering as an affirmative answer; and then indeed he will experience all the benefits of appearing before the king, of breathing the atmosphere of the court, and of conversing with superior excellence. Even so he who prays—fully believing that God waits to hear and says, What is thy petition, and what is thy request—*he* will come into the presence of the King of kings, and even though his particular request should not be granted, he will go away awed and purified from that presence, his very person ennobled by such communion, and his face shining with light from heaven. It was in just this way that the Westminster Assembly of Divines were elevated, and almost inspired, to indite that remarkable answer to the question, "What is God?" in the catechism. To define God! how extremely difficult! how utterly impossible! It were to comprehend the Infinite in the finite. The grandeur of the subject lifted them above themselves. But they felt the need of special divine illumination. They believed in the efficacy of prayer. They rose to ask for divine teaching, and felt themselves transported almost into the presence of the infinite Spirit. And no sooner did they look up than light from the Throne beamed upon their understandings and their hearts. No sooner did he who led their devotions—the youngest of the number—open his mouth to speak unto God, than it was filled by God himself; and the first words that he uttered were an invocation to the Deity, which they pronounced by acclamation to comprise the answer they sought, and which is probably the best answer to that great question that was ever compassed in words of merely human wisdom.

Such then is prayer. It is literally *asking that we may receive.* It recognizes God as one who hears prayer, and who invites and commands all men to pray with the expectation of being heard,—who says to every believing Christian, nay, to every humble and penitent sinner: Ask what I shall give thee—and whose veracity is therefore pledged to grant us our requests if we ask what is agreeable to his will. And it is just this *pledge* of the divine *veracity* on which rests the assurance that God *will* hear and answer prayer.

God has actually given such a pledge. He has given it in a great variety of forms and ways. He has given it in all the ways in which he has invited men to pray, and encouraged the hope that prayer will not be unavailing. He has given it in his works and in his word. He has written it in the soul of man as well as on the pages of the Bible. He has repeated it in times and ways without number, now in inarticulate sighs from within the soul, now in loud voices from external nature—at one time by the mouth of prophets and apostles and all his faithful ministers, at another by the secret whispers of his Holy Spirit. And will he prove false to his word, so solemnly plighted, so often and so distinctly repeated ?

The instincts of the lower animals, the appetences of plants even, are unerring. They never mislead or disappoint the humblest of God's creatures. The pale and delicate plant, that grows in a dark cell, bends its stalk and stretches out its leaves towards the narrow grated window, and *finds* the light which it seeks. And shall the feeble and humble soul that lives in the prison of this world, grope for the light of heaven, reach after it, long for it, pray for it, and no light be given it ? The slender and flexible vine sends forth its tendrils for some arbor or trellis, shrub or tree, about which they may twine and gain support ; and it finds just the support it needs. Shall the penitent and believing soul, then, not find the support which it almost instinctively seeks in God, which it almost necessarily hopes to lay hold of by prayer, and prayer alone ? All animals are formed with a physical structure adapted to breathing and seeing, and when, in accordance with the unconscious impulses of their nature, they expand their lungs, though it be for the first time, they breathe in the vital air ; when they open their eyes, they see the pleasant light of the sun. In like manner, all mankind are made with a spiritual nature, which, more or less strongly and distinctly, impels them to pray, and that with the hope of receiving the things for which they pray (for the belief that prayer will be heard and answered is as instinctive and universal as is the impulse which prompts to prayer). Now, shall this higher spiritual impulse alone disappoint and deceive? Shall this alone prove delusive, and find no corresponding objective reality? Shall the soul expand its desires towards God, and inhale no breath from heaven? Shall the soul lift up its prayer for special divine teaching, and no light from heaven greet those longing eyes? The Lord satisfieth the desire of every living thing with food suited to its nature and necessities; and when his *children* open their *hearts* and wait for him to fill them, shall they be sent away empty? Or if they ask of him a fish, will he give them a serpent; or if they ask an egg, will he give them a scorpion? When they ask of him substantial and satisfying food, will he give them only vapor and moonshine, and all such transcendental stuff as dreams are made of, or bid them be content with the intrinsic satisfaction of asking, and the incidental benefits of coming before him with their requests?

It is with sorrow and shame that we resort to such arguments, and dwell on them so long to prove a point, which, to the simple, unsophisticated and believing spirit, must be so clear and plain in the light of Scripture and experience. But ours is a day of philosophy and speculation, rather than simple faith. There is now a strong propensity to sink the supernatural and special in the natural and ordinary; to reduce even miracles and prophecies to the sway of law and the rank of common events; to resolve all the phenomena of the objective creation and the very existence and agency of the Creator into the subjective qualities and workings of the human soul. And while the pantheistic school of philosophers have thus made God the creature of the human mind, instead of the human mind the creature of God, and the rationalists have reduced the inspiration of the Scriptures to a level with the imaginations of the poet and the intuitions of the philosopher, evangelical Christians are in danger of divesting prayer of its most sacred and divine prerogatives, and expecting its chief benefits as the natural result of the operations of their own souls, rather than as a free gift direct from the throne of the Most High. In such an age, we feel constrained to remind believers as well as unbelievers, that God *never proves false* to the lowest instinct of his humblest creatures; and it is quite incredible that he should disappoint the higher instincts or intuitions which he has wrought into the souls of men. He has impressed on the human heart every where an intuitive conviction of his existence and providence and moral government; and he *does* exist, not merely as the co-eternal soul of the world, but as a provident Father and righteous moral Governor of the universe. He has led all men in all nations and ages to expect a supernatural revelation, and to believe in a special divine *inspiration* as an essential *characteristic* of such a revelation; and in the fulness of times he gave the world the Scriptures of the Old and New Testament, bearing all the marks of an extraordinary and infallible inspiration. In like manner, he has prompted men every where to pray, with the expectation of receiving in return that for which they pray ; and who that is a believer in the divine existence and in revelation,—who that recognizes the veracity of God wherever and however plighted to any of his creatures, can doubt that he will fully redeem his pledge to hear prayer ?

With our confidence in the divine veracity thus established, let us now proceed to consider, with some care, what God has *said* in his Word touching the efficacy of prayer. Nature teaches us to expect that prayer will be heard ; the Scriptures *assure* us that it *will* be. In how many places and how many ways is the veracity of God pledged directly or indirectly in his Word, that he will hear and answer prayer ! In how many passages of Holy Writ—passages almost without number—is the certain efficacy and great power of prayer asserted or implied ? It is implied in the innumerable invitations and commands to pray ; to pray always with all prayer and supplication,—to pray without ceasing, and never faint,—of which the Bible is full ; for what are such invitations and commands but hypocrisy and mockery, if prayer is of no avail to secure the blessings for which we ask ? It is yet more forcibly inculcated in the severe rebukes which are often administered to those who cast off fear and restrain prayer, and who say : "What profit shall we have, if we pray unto him ?" It is clearly taught in those numerous passages which impute our destitution of spiritual blessings not to God's unwillingness to hear prayer, but to our not offering prayer, or not offering it aright: "Ye are not straitened in me; ye are straitened in your own bowels. Ye have not, because ye ask not; ye ask and receive not, because ye ask amiss." It is expressly declared in passages not a few, where it is the direct object of the sacred writer to insist on the efficacy of prayer: "The effectual, fervent prayer of the righteous man availeth much." "The Lord is nigh unto all them that call upon him, to all that call upon him in truth." "He will fulfil the desire of them that fear him; he also will hear their cry, and save them." It is contained in many great and precious promises, addressed directly to those who offer prayer: "Ask, and it shall be given you; seek, and ye shall find; knock, and it shall be opened unto you.' The reasonableness of the doctrine is *argued*, and the appeal is made to our own willingness, as parents, to grant the requests of our children, feeble and imperfect as our own parental love is, in comparison with that of the infinite and universal Parent: "If ye then, being evil, know how to give good gifts to your children, how much more shall your Father who is in heaven give good things to them that ask him?" Nay, reference is even made to the power of importunate entreaties to move the hearts and wills of the *selfish* and the *unjust*, in order to set forth the certainty that the prayers of his children will not be unheeded by him who cannot be unjust, and whose nature is love. Most frequently and most powerfully is the doctrine taught in that most efficacious of all ways of teaching, by example. Time would fail us to enumerate a small fraction only of the many,

many instances on record, in which God *has* heard his servants when they have cried unto him, and sent them the very blessing which they needed, and for which they prayed. There is no kind or degree of blessing, great or small, temporal or spiritual, which has not been borne on the wings of prayer from heaven to earth. There is no time or place, or form or manner of prayer, private or public, by day or by night, in the house of God or at the family altar, on the housetop or by the sea-shore, for one's self or for one's friends and neighbors, or for the church, or for the world, that has not been heard and answered. From the intercession of Abraham for the cities of the plain, as recorded in the book of Genesis, to the unceasing prayers of the whole church in the Acts of the Apostles, what is the history of the Old Testament and of the New, but a record of life and death, of blessing and cursing, suspended on the prayers of God's people ?

The course of nature, the vicissitudes of the seasons, the power of the winds and waves, and all the elements, have been directed and controlled by prayer. Prayer saved the lives of shipwrecked mariners, brought up the rebellious, but penitent prophet, from the bottom of the sea, as from the depths of hell ; called down fire from heaven to consume the offering on the altar of the living God ; spread famine and pestilence over the guilty land, and in due time stayed their ravages ; shut up the windows of heaven that it might not rain for long years of drought, and then opened them again, and the heavens gave rain, and the earth yielded her increase. The destruction or preservation

2*

of cities, the victory or defeat of armies, the rise and fall of nations, as well as the life and death of individuals, were suspended on prayer. Prayer carried back the shadow on the dial ten degrees, and added fifteen years to the good king's life. Prayer stood between the living and the dead, and stayed the destroyer's march through the camp of Israel. Again, prayer sent forth the destroyer into the camp of the enemies of Israel, and one night extinguished the whole army; in the morning, they were all dead corpses. Prayer fed the hungry and clothed the naked, and comforted the widow and blessed the fatherless, and healed the sick and raised the dead. Prayer saved Nineveh from destruction, and would have saved Sodom, had there been in it ten righteous persons. Prayer averted or delayed many a threatened evil from the chosen people of God, and delivered them from the hand of many an oppressor; and brought them back from their captivity in Babylon, and rebuilt their temple, and would have saved them from the final extinction of their national existence, if they had but united in humble and penitent deprecation of divine justice. Prayer shut the mouths of lions, quenched the violence of fire, opened the doors of prisons, and, knocking off their chains, bade the prisoners go free.

The prosperity of true religion, the edification of the church, and the conversion of sinners, have always and every where been connected with, and proportioned to, the prayers of the faithful. "Lord, revive thy work," was the prayer of prophets and ancient saints; and the Lord revived his work, and lifted upon them the light of his countenance ; and he that went forth weeping, bearing precious seed, came again with rejoicing, bringing his sheaves with him. The apostles and primitive Christians waited at Jerusalem, and pleaded in united, earnest and importunate prayer the promised gift of the Holy Spirit, which alone could endue them with power for their work ; and while they were yet all with one accord in one place, the promise was fulfilled ; the rushing, mighty wind, which symbolized the heavenly influence, filled the house ; the cloven tongues, like as of fire, which were so significant at once of the purifying and the miraculous power of the Spirit, sat upon each of them : and the same day, there were added unto them about three thousand converts from the unbelieving and lately persecuting multitude. And as they afterwards continued instant in prayer and Christian communion, "the Lord added to them daily of such as should be saved." Prayer and the ministry of the Word were the combined instrumentalities on which the apostles relied for the upbuilding of the church and the salvation of souls ; the preached Word as the means of reaching the hearts and consciences of men ; the prayer as the means of bringing down the blessing of God, without which even the good seed sown by the apostles could yield no increase. Prayer and a holy life and conversation were also the main resources on which common Christians depended for their own progressive sanctification and the conviction and conversion of their unbelieving neighbors ; these were the weapons of their warfare, and the pillars of their strength ; these the vital breath of their souls, and the daily business of their lives.

Prayer then has ever been a *ruling power* in the history of the church and of the world, as that history has been written by the finger of God himself. He has promised to hear prayer, and he has fulfilled the promise. He has pledged himself in every possible way to grant the requests of his people, and he has fully redeemed the pledge. He has taken great pains so to speak, by repeated promises and renewed pledges, by solemn asseverations and cogent arguments, and earnest appeals and forcible illustrations, and unquestionable facts to encourage men to prayer; and he has taken no less pains not to disappoint the hopes and expectations he has thus raised. He has ever been saying, "Ask what I shall give thee," and ever been giving, what men have truly and properly asked. He has invited his people to *command* him—he has permitted them to reason and expostulate and wrestle with him, as it were, in prayer; and so far from being displeased with their boldness, when they have said, "I will not let thee go without a blessing," he has rewarded the boldest confidence with the richest gifts. Jacob wrestled with God till the break of day, and then received the name of *Israel*, because, "as a prince, he had power with God, and prevailed;" and the people of God's choice and covenant and grace, have ever since not only borne his better than royal name, but inherited his more than princely power. They are still God's spiritual *Israel*—they still *have power with God, and prevail.* They still have access to him who is the Angel of the Covenant, and influence with him, who is not only Head of the church, but Head over all things to the church, and has all power on earth and in heaven. They still move the arm that moves and governs the Universe.

Prayer may well be said to *rule* in the kingdom of nature, the kingdom of providence, and the kingdom grace, for it has influence with him who is king in all these kingdoms. It touches and sways the sceptre of the King of kings, the Lord of heaven and earth. It was so settled in the counsels of eternity. It was God's eternal purpose to bestow rich and manifold blessings on mankind, but it was his eternal purpose also to confer them only in answer to prayer. His truth has long been pledged in his word, by many precious promises, to do great things for his people; but he will yet be "inquired" of by his people to do for them these very things which he has thus explicitly promised. Prayer thus enters, as it were, into the very *plan* and *structure* of the *universe.* It is, if we may so speak, one of the elementary principles, or forces, in the original constitution of things —not less so than light, or heat, or gravitation, or electricity. It is an invisible, intangible principle; but so are they. It cannot be weighed or measured; neither can they. The material world was made for moral ends, and moral elements enter, as it were, into its composition—moral forces mould, so to speak, its masses, direct its movements, and control the course of events. And among these prayer is perhaps the chief.

The frame of nature was so constituted at the

first, or, (if any prefer another mode of conceiving and representing the same essential truth), its course is so directed, that it always harmonizes and falls in with the fervent, effectual prayers of righteous men; and when the sun sheds its quickening beams, or the rain descends in fertilizing showers, or drought, or famine, or pestilence is averted in accordance with the united and believing prayers of a prostrate church and nation, there is every reason to believe that the prayers are as efficacious and as essential to the results, as the natural causes; and the efficacy of both is alike provided for in the nature of things—alike contemplated and involved in the plans of Him who worketh all things according to the counsel of His own will. He would as soon give the rain (in such a case) without the clouds, or the electric fluid, as without the prayers of his people. To dispense with either the material, or the moral instrumentality, were alike to sever the established order of sequences, and violate the ordinances of Heaven.

Still more palpably does prayer enter into the economy of divine Providence and divine grace. The efficacy of prayer is one of the great fixed facts and established laws of God's providential and moral government, which he will no more supersede or dispense with, than he will contravene the laws of his own existence and agency, or the free moral agency of his intelligent creatures. Prayer and pains go hand in hand in the accomplishment of the greatest events in human life; and what God hath thus joined together, man cannot put asunder Prayer and medicines,—prayer and means,—are often seen to co-operate marvellously in the cure of diseases, whether in the natural body or the body politic : and who can say, that the means are any more essential, or the medicines any more effective, than the prayers? Prayer enters as an essential element into the happiness of the individual, the well-being of the community, and the prosperity of the nation. So it was in the history of the Israelites,—so it was in the history of the Pilgrim Fathers of New England. Mather's Magnalia is a record and testimony to the efficacy of prayer, scarcely less striking than the historical books of the Bible. Famine and pestilence, and war and captivity were averted; health and plenty, and liberty and peace, were secured in almost visible answers to prayer. And though it is less manifest, the truth is no less real in our own day, and if our prayers were equally importunate, and our faith equally strong, we should see no less convincing demonstrations of the power of prayer in averting social and civil evils, and in procuring national and providential blessings—we should see, almost as with the bodily eye, prayer taking hold of the arm of Providence, and that arm, in consequence, laid bare and stretched out in all the great events of our national history, so that we could no more doubt that prayer is a great power among the nations, than we could disbelieve the doctrine of an overruling Providence, or the existence of the law of gravitation.

Above all, prayer is a great power in the church and in the hearts of men. Prayer brings down the

Spirit of God to enlighten the darkness of nature, to convince the world of sin, to lead sinners to repentance, and the remission of their sins; to dwell in the church, and in the hearts of all true believers. Here, above all, the power of God is linked to the weakness of men; the riches of God waits for the requests of men; the sovereignty of God invites the commands of men. Here is the point to which all the designs of nature and Providence tend; towards which all material elements and forces converge; in which all historical events culminate. The material was made for the spiritual; the world was made, and is preserved for the church; and if prayer is a controlling force in the former, it is doubly so in the latter. God in Christ reigns in nature and Providence for the *benefit* of the *church;* and if all the resources of his wisdom and power wait on prayer in his natural and providential government, it is chiefly intended to subserve and to illustrate the greater riches and resources of his grace, in doing for the *church* exceeding abundantly above what they can ask or even think. The history of Israel in the Old Testament was a type of the Christian church in the New Testament; and even the miraculous power of prayer and faith in the primitive church was symbolic of the more enduring, and in some respects, more important spiritual energies that still reside in the prayers of the Christian church.

So far from considering the law of prayer to be repealed, or its power diminished, we should expect its mightiest energies to be developed, and its most marvellous triumphs displayed in these latter days, on which the ends of the world are come. So the Scriptures teach. They forbid us to look upon prophets and apostles as men of a different nature from ourselves, so exalted above meaner mortals as to be no examples for us. They tell us that even Elias was a man of like passions with ourselves, and they tell us this for the express purpose of encouraging *us* to hope for like answers to our prayers. While we stand wondering at the miracles of the apostles, and, with the polytheistic Lycaonians, are almost ready to offer sacrifices to them, as to superior beings, they take pains to assure us that they are ordinary men, and that this is only the power of God intrusted to them in answer to prayer.

The promises of Christ to hear prayer are expressly extended to the end of the world; and as all the past victories of the church have been triumphs of prayer, so we cannot doubt the final and decisive victory of the Captain of our salvation over the powers of darkness (as the result of which Satan will be bound a thousand years), will be a more impressive demonstration than has ever yet been seen, of the moral omnipotence of prayer. The leaders and captains of the Lord's host in that day will pray to the Lord Jehovah, and their hands will be stayed up by the faith and prayer of the priests of the people; and the enemies of Israel and Israel's God will meet with an irrecoverable overthrow. The prophets of that day will pray to the God of grace, and the heavens will be opened, and the Spirit will descend in copious showers, and righteousness shall flow as a river, and salvation as the waves of the sea. The apostles of that day will pray to the Head of the church, who is also Head over all things, and the morally impotent man shall walk and leap for joy, and the spiritually blind shall see, and the dead in trespasses and sins shall rise to a new and holy life. The whole church of that day shall be with one accord in every part of the world waiting and praying for the promised Spirit for the world's conversion, and (though no audible sound may be heard, and no rushing mighty wind shake the places in which they are assembled) the Spirit shall take possession of their hearts, and fill the whole earth, and (though no visible appearance of cloven tongues, like as of fire, may be seen) the hearts of men shall glow with holy love, and their tongues shall speak an unknown language, even the language of heaven. Then will be realized and consummated all and more than all that the soul of man has longed for, and the course of nature has typified, and the interpositions of Providence have promised, and the Scriptures have recorded or predicted, of the mighty power of prayer.

But that consummation, so devoutly to be wished, is inseparably connected in the purpose and promise of God (and therefore in the essential constitution of things and the necessary course of events), inseparably connected with the effectual, fervent prayers of his people. Effectual fervent prayer, together with the corresponding exertions which cannot fail to accompany such prayer—effectual prayer and faithful preaching by the ministry—fervent prayer and holy living in the church—these are the appointed means of which that consummation is the certain result ; these the necessary antecedent, of which that is the infallible consequent ; these the indispensable condition, without which that can no more be accomplished than an effect can be produced without a cause. As well might there be vegetation without rain or sunshine, as well might there be reaping without sowing, and wealth without industry or health, and strength without activity, as the revival of religion, the salvation of souls, and the conversion of the world, without the required measure of prayer, as well as efforts and sacrifices on the part of Christians and Christian ministers. The promises of God all rest on this express condition. On this condition, and this only, is his veracity pledged for the bestowment of the promised blessings. We have his promissory note, signed with his own hand, his solemn bond sealed with his own seal in the presence of many witnesses. But it is *conditional*, and without the performance of the conditions on our part, it binds him no more than so much blank paper.

Under such circumstances, to impute to him the failure of the promised blessings, or entertain the slightest question of his veracity in any the remotest corner of our hearts, is to charge him with our own unfaithfulness. Nay, "let God be true, and every man a liar." "We receive not, because we ask not, or we ask amiss, that we may consume it on our lusts." Shall we still further add insult to injury by making him a liar, and holding him responsible for our own sins ? Let us first bring all the tithes into the storehouse. Then he invites and commands us to prove him, to put his veracity to the test, and see if he will not open the windows of heaven and pour us out a blessing, such that there shall not be room enough to receive it.

What a fearful responsibility is devolved on us, in that *we* are *now* intrusted with the power of prayer! Was ever such a privilege, such a possession, such a power, placed in the hands of mortal men? And was ever property so undervalued, in our day at least; was ever privilege so slighted and abused; was ever power so wasted, neglected and despised? Perhaps nothing so illustrates and enforces the *duty* of prayer as the *power* of prayer. What *right* have we to leave unappropriated and unapplied, a power which God has appointed for the salvation of men, which Christians in former ages have wielded with such magnificent effect, and which God and man, heaven and earth, now wait to see *us* put forth for the world's redemption? The question, which at the close of the previous chapter pressed with such weight upon the consciences of professed Christians, here returns with double emphasis: What "inhumanity to man," and what want of sympathy with God and Christ, are chargeable upon us, if after all that has been done and suffered and sacrificed by God the Father, the Son, and the Holy Spirit, to open the way for the efficacy of prayer, and the salvation of men, we fail to offer the effectual, fervent prayer of the righteous man in such manner and measure, as alone, according to the divine plan, can render these sufferings and sacrifices efficacious!

CHAPTER III.

Believing Prayer the great Desideratum of the Church in our Day—"When the Son of Man cometh, shall he find Faith on the Earth?"—Too much occasion to ask this pathetic question now—The Promise of our Lord unlimited in its terms: "All things whatsoever ye shall ask in Prayer, believing, ye shall receive"—To be taken with certain obvious Limitations—With these Limitations, the promise verified, not only to Apostles, but to Common Christians, according to their Faith—The Power of Miracles only symbolic of the Perpetual Power of Faith and Prayer in the Spiritual World—But this power not usually appropriated, or even aspired to by the Church now—Exceptions—But these only prove the rule—The Church has many Wants, but wants nothing so much as a revival of the primitive spirit of Faith and Prayer.

IN the parable of the unjust judge, which is designed to teach that "men ought always to pray and not to faint," after the most convincing demonstration that God will interpose in behalf of his "elect, who cry day and night unto him," our Lord concludes with this searching inquiry: "*Nevertheless*"—notwithstanding the irresistible evidence, the absolute certainty of this interposition—"NEVERTHELESS, when the Son of Man cometh, shall he find faith on the earth?" Of all the touching and pathetic appeals that fell from the lips of him, who spake as never man spake, none is more touching, none more pathetic, than this, unless it be the severe, yet tender reproof, which he addressed to his disciples, when amid his agony in the garden, he returned, and found them sleeping: "What! could ye not watch with me one hour?" And it may perhaps be doubted, whether it was not even more trying to the Saviour's heart—a heart which craved not only the steadfast affection, but the unwavering confidence of his disciples—to know that his word would be so generally discredited by his disciples in later times, than it was to find himself forsaken by his immediate followers in that hour of brief, though peculiar trial. Nothing so offends man, nothing so dishonors God, as to question his veracity. And if Jesus, who is both God and man, cannot be honored by the implicit confidence, as well as the supreme love of those for whom he died, nothing else on earth is of any value to him, and he loses the very object for which he came into the world.

And yet how many are there in our day that are willing to take him at his word, and expect the fulfilment of his promise in regard to prayer, in its obvious intent, as he uttered it with his own lips, and left it on record in his gospel?

The promise, as we read it in the gospels, is absolute and unlimited: "All things whatsoever ye shall ask in prayer, believing, ye shall receive;" or, as it is in another Evangelist: "What things soever ye desire when ye pray, believe that ye receive them, and ye shall have them." Of course this, like all the other promises and precepts of the gospel (which are usually expressed in singularly bold and unguarded language), must be taken with such limitations as are necessarily involved in the nature of the case. The prayer must be real prayer, the faith must be genuine and well-grounded faith, and the objects must be proper objects of desire ; or, as the Apostle John defines them, "things according to the will of God." For this is only saying that the faith must be such faith as the disciples of Christ might be expected to exercise, the prayer such prayer as they would be likely to offer, and the objects such objects as they would naturally and reasonably desire, *under the divine teaching of his Word and Spirit.* Without such limitations, the promise was not fulfilled to the very chief of the apostles. With these necessary and obvious limitations, it was literally and gloriously fulfilled to the entire body of the primitive disciples. And in their undoubting reliance on this promise, in their habitual use of this divine weapon, lay the secret of their strength, and the certainty of their triumph. By this they wrought those signs and wonders which struck the senses of the multitude ; and by this they achieved those greater miracles of moral power, and saving mercy, which subdued the hearts of the people.

With the same, or similar limitations,—that is, such as grow obviously and necessarily out of the nature of the case, and the circumstances of the times,—the promise is just as real, just as literal, just as reliable, just as full of truth and power now, as it ever was. All things whatsoever that *we* ask in real prayer, and genuine, well-grounded faith, according to the will of God, we shall receive. In other words, whatever we ask under the divine teaching and influence of the truth and the Spirit of Christ, will surely be granted. The promise is not obsolete, its power is not extinguished, or even impaired. There is nothing in its terms to limit it to the apostles or the primitive church ; neither is there in the nature of the case. Inspiration has indeed ceased, but spiritual illumination may, and often does, and should every where, take its place. Signs and wonders have come to an end, but moral miracles may be, and should be of every-day occurrence. We cannot be supernaturally inspired to utter a word which shall, with infallible certainty, be followed by the exertion of a supernatural power ; but we can be divinely moved to the use of means, which we are authorized confidently to expect will be accompanied by a divine energy ; we can be taught by the Spirit of God to offer prayers, which we may be sure God will answer, by granting our requests. "*Delight thyself in the Lord,* and he will" *still* "give thee the desires of thy heart." "Have faith in God," live in habitual *sympathy* and communion with him, and mountains of difficulty and opposition shall be removed out of the way. "*If ye abide in me, and my words abide in you,* ye shall ask what ye will, and it shall be done unto you." The time may be delayed, the manner may be unexpected, but sooner or later, in some form or other, the answer is sure to come. Not a tear of sacred sorrow, not a breath of holy desire, poured out in prayer to God, will ever be lost ; but, in God's own best time and way, it will be wafted back again in clouds of mercy, and fall in showers of blessing on you and those for whom you pray.

The manner may be different now from what it was in the Old Testament or in the New ; but the principle, the spirit, the power is the same. We cannot talk with God face to face like Abraham, nor open and shut the heavens like Elijah ; nor heal the sick, and raise the dead, like Peter and John and Paul. But our importunate intercessions may save many a Sodom from temporal and eternal destruction ; and our oft-repeated supplications, bowing ourselves low in the dust seven times before the Lord, though at the seventh time the only favorable sign shall be a cloud no bigger than a man's hand, may bring down copious showers of spiritual, aye, and temporal blessings, on the parched places of the earth ; and our prayer of faith may heal the sick, and the Lord shall even raise up those who are quite dead in trespasses and sins. The most marvellous displays of divine power that ever attended on the word of prophets and apostles are but the *symbols* of the moral and spiritual power of believing prayer in our age, and only *shadows* of still greater and better things that are to come in the last days.

Thus sure is the word of promise to us and our children ; thus mighty is the power of prayer in our day ; *nevertheless*, as the Son of Man looks down upon the churches, does he find faith on the earth ? Alas ! ours is an unbelieving age ; an age of skepticism in the world, and feeble faith in the church, and therefore of weakness in all high moral and spiritual enterprises. So far from leaning on the promise of Christ as our staff, and wielding it as the weapon of our spiritual power, we generally regard it as obsolete, meant only for apostles, or, at most, the primitive Christians, and of use now only to be hung up among other an-

3

tiquities of the church, like rusty pieces of antiquated armor, in proof that "there were giants in those days."

True, we meet with now and then a poor widow who trusts the promise of God in little and great things, and never doubts that *all* will be well with her and her fatherless children. And according to her faith, so it is unto her. Her cruse of oil is never empty, her barrel of meal never fails. Never a want of her life is left unsupplied, never a desire of her heart but is sooner or later gratified, even as never a doubt clouds her belief that the Lord will provide. Here and there "a *mother in Israel*," too, takes God at his word, and labors and prays for individual after individual in her class, and for one class after another in her Sabbath-school, till every individual of every class that has passed under her instructions is hopefully converted; and when at length, full of years and of labors, she ceases from her work, she has the unspeakable happiness not only of seeing her own children walking in the truth, and filling stations of eminent usefulness, but of knowing that her spiritual children are multiplied and scattered, like good seed, broadcast over the land. Sometimes a Mary Lyon is raised up with faith enough to found Holyoke Seminary, in the face of an unbelieving church and a sneering world, and with prayer enough to secure a special revival of religion in it every year of her life. The secret of those wonderful revivals was never understood till after her death, when they were found, in almost every instance, to have been preceded by special seasons of persevering secret prayer. She was as remarkable for faith and prayer as she was for benevolence and untiring energy ; she expected great things, she attempted great things, and, with the blessing of Heaven, she accomplished great things for the education of her sex and the redemption of mankind. And not a few of that class of women, of whom Paul speaks with honor, as "caring for the things of the Lord," but whom the world seldom names except in terms of reproach, will be found to have "their names written in heaven," as those who, while they blessed mankind by their self-denying charities, have "had power with God, and prevailed" in believing prayer.

Now and then a layman in the church, as he follows his daily occupation, makes a business also of conversing on personal religion with those who fall in his way, and are associated with him, and at the same time bears them on the arms of faith and prayer continually ; and though his life, like his Master's, is short, his reward, like his, is great, and he goes up to cast at his Redeemer's feet a crown jewelled with scores, perhaps hundreds, of precious souls. Now and then a young man in college believes in the efficacy of prayer and corresponding effort for the conversion of his classmates and companions in study, and he does more good in college than most educated men do in a long life.

Now and then a minister of the gospel enters into the very spirit of the Redeemer's promise. He does not surpass his ministerial brethren, perhaps is inferior to many of them, in talents and literary attainments. But he baptizes every sermon with prayer, and leavens every conversation with faith. He "goeth forth and weepeth, bearing precious seed;" every kernel seems to fall on good ground, and all the ground is moistened with the dews and rains of heaven; and ever and anon, he "comes again with rejoicing, bringing his sheaves with him." But he is regarded as a kind of prodigy, that hardly belongs to this world; at best, as a miracle and an anomaly in the present age; and he is looked on not only with wonder for his success, but with some doubts of his orthodoxy, and not a few fears for his audacity. His people, who have learned from their pastor to be "strong in faith, giving glory to God," are a sort of oasis in the desert, wet habitually with copious dews, like Gideon's fleece, while all is dry around them. They enjoy a perpetual revival, while others, only on rare occasions, catch their spirit of believing prayer, and share in their spiritual blessings. As they are honored with the constant presence of the Spirit of God here, so hereafter such a minister and his people will shine together "as the brightness of the firmament, and as the stars for ever and ever."

The late venerable Dr. Judson was a rare example of close approximation to apostolic faith and power. Not satisfied with translating the Scriptures into the language of the Burmans, he was intent on preaching the gospel with his own lips where no one else would penetrate. The jungles of the Karens rose up and called him blessed, and the wilderness blossomed before him as the rose. He was pre-eminently a man of prayer, and in a good old age, he bore this testimony to the faithfulness of a prayer-hearing and covenant-keeping God: "I never was deeply interested in any object, I never prayed sincerely and earnestly for any thing, but it came; at some time—no matter at how distant a day—somehow, in some shape, probably the last I should have devised, it came."* And yet even Judson was "frightened" at the seeming audacity of such an assertion, and hardly knew whether the weakness or the boldness of his faith were the more deserving of reproof.

In short, all these sketches (which we have drawn from real life, though only in two or three instances have we mentioned names) are so manifestly exceptions, that they only prove the rule. They demonstrate the power of a primitive faith, but they also mark by contrast the feebleness of an unbelieving and degenerate age. Faith is the exception, the rule is unbelief. We can only touch upon a few of the leading facts that substantiate this proposition. Nor need we. It stands proved and confessed in the very wonder with which we look back upon the faith of the primitive church as purely miraculous, and in the mingled distrust and amazement with which we regard the like faith in those exceptional cases which do occur in modern times, as deluded enthusiasm, or at best unwarranted presumption. We do not even aspire to such honor and power with God, but frankly and freely disavow all right and title to it.

The members of the primitive church, "all with one accord in one place," waited in earnest, importu-

* Memoir by Dr. Wayland, vol. ii., p. 37.

nate and believing prayer, till they were endued with power for the arduous work of saving a world wholly given up to idolatry. Where is such a prayer-meeting to be found now-a-days—*all with one accord in one place?* And where is such waiting seen—waiting for the providence and the Spirit of God, not to do their work for them, but to work in and by them, and give them a power which nothing could gainsay or resist? There is enough waiting for divine sovereignty to do its own work without human agency, and there is much running of human agency without being divinely commissioned or empowered. But where is that beautiful *union* of waiting and running, and that harmonious *co*-operation of human instrumentality and divine efficiency, which so marked and energized and blessed the primitive church?

The seven deacons of the church at Jerusalem were *all* "men full of faith and the Holy Ghost." Where now is the church that is blessed with such a deaconry, or even such a ministry? Nay, too many churches now-a-days do not even *aspire* to the possession of such officers. They do not *ask* in reference to a *minister* even, "Is he a man of piety and prayer? is he full of faith and the Holy Ghost?" but, "Is he a smart man? is he a good speaker? has he a fine voice and manner and person? will he sell the pews, and build up the society?" *They* cannot be expected to pray, certainly not in public; it is for this very purpose that they hire their *minister*. If they go to the prayer-meeting, it is only on condition that the minister shall do all the praying as well as all the talking. If they desire to see conversions in the house of God, they expect them to be the results of their pastor's preaching and not of their prayers. How unlike the lay-ministry, "the royal priesthood," that made up the primitive church, who, while permitted to remain at Jerusalem, prayed without ceasing, and when scattered by persecution, went every where preaching the word! Even the missionary concert has degenerated very much into a lecture-room for the communication of missionary intelligence, and the conversion of the world is to be accomplished by machinery, and money and men, rather than by the power of God sent down from heaven in answer to prayer.

Ministers themselves fall in with the current, and wear themselves out in the preparation of polished sermons, with too little prayer for the presence of that Spirit who alone can give power to a sermon, either in the composition or the delivery. Colleges and Theological Seminaries are strongly tempted to meet the popular demand with a corresponding supply, and bend their energies too exclusively to the education of accomplished scholars and eloquent orators for the pulpit, perchance for mere secular employments, while the heart, the seat of all life and power, is comparatively neglected.

When the church and the ministry are so secularized in matters properly religious, it is hardly to be expected that they will carry much of the power of prayer or vital godliness into political and public affairs. Their weapons are too often not spiritual, mighty through God, but carnal, and all too weak to pull down the strongholds of corruption and oppression in high places. Not that they send too many petitions to their civil rulers, but they carry too few to the throne of Him who ruleth on earth and in heaven. Not that they vote or agitate too much. Far from it. It is their sacred duty to vote. Agitation is essential to the purity, nay, to the vitality of the moral and political atmosphere. But they *rely* too much on voting and agitating, too little on unceasing prayer in private and in public, in the family, in the social circle, and in the house of God.

We say these things in sorrow, not in anger, nor in the spirit of censoriousness. Croaking, like birds of evil omen, is our utter abhorrence. But we are painfully convinced of the truth and necessity of what we have said, therefore have we spoken. The house of God, the prayer-meeting, the closets, and the consciences of Christians, do they not all bear witness to a sad dereliction of duty in this respect? We need more money and more men, we need more activity and more benevolence, we need better teachers and better preachers; but we need nothing so much as a revival of the primitive spirit of faith and prayer in the churches. We need to be converted, and become as little children, in the simplicity of our trust and confidence. Then should we know the meaning of Christian "*bravery*," of Christian "*gladness* and singleness of heart." Faith is courage. Faith is power, and want of faith is weakness. It is so in every thing. It is emphatically so in religion. Christians can be strong only in faith and prayer. If weak here, the right arm of their strength is broken, and they can expect nothing but shameful discomfiture in the end of all their enterprises. Unless Christians can be stirred up, and that speedily, to more earnest, constant and believing prayer for the church, the country and the world, and especially for our colleges; in which, as we shall now endeavor to show, the hopes of the church, the country and the world, all centre; worldliness and ungodliness will continue to come in like a flood, sweeping away the dearest interests of men for this life, and their brightest hopes for the next, till at length, in answer to the supplications of a *more prayerful and believing* age, the Spirit of God shall lift up a standard against them. God will never honor those that will not honor him; and he will never repeal that great law of his spiritual kingdom: "BE IT UNTO THEE ACCORDING TO THY FAITH."

CHAPTER IV.

Colleges—Their Origin, Design, and History—English in their Germ, but American in their Development—The College not a University—More like Eton, Rugby, and the German Gymnasia—An Educational Institution—Self-educated Men conscious of their Deficiencies—Franklin, Washington, Clay—College Studies—College Officers—Students discipline each other—Rise and Progress of American Colleges—College Education the established Policy of the American People—An essential Element in American Society—Educates the Leading Minds—The right Age—A sort of Family Organization—Parental Government and Influence—Colleges are Permanent Foundations, and tend to perpetuate an Educated Ministry, Magistracy, &c.—The Keystone of our Educational System, and the Cornerstone of our Institutions—The enlightened Christian and Patriot cannot but pray for these Foundations of Many Generations.

OUR educational, like our political and religious institutions, were derived, though not servilely copied, from those of the mother country; and the former, not less than the latter, were coeval with our national existence. It is a striking characteristic of American history, that it cannot, like that of the nations of the Old World, be traced back to an obscure and barbarous antiquity. Born and nurtured beneath the bright light of Christianity and modern civilization, it has, from the first, been "known and read of all men;" and from the first, it has been a history of law and order, of light and knowledge, of well-organized and well-sustained literary, as well as political and religious institutions.

Our system of college education is English in its

germ, but American in its development. Like the American people, it has cast off the bondage of prescription and the unbending rigidity of English institutions, and put on a flexibility suited to the altered circumstances of a young nation in a new world. It has not, however, cut loose from the past. It has not broken away from all respect for time-honored usages and pursuits. At once conservative and progressive in its spirit, it strives to preserve a due medium between a bigoted attachment to all that is old, and an indiscriminate passion for all that is new. Not less scientific than classical in its course of studies, it aims to engraft the science of the moderns on the wisdom of the ancients. Its anchor takes firm hold on the past, but its sails are set, and its prow directed to a more brilliant future.

An American college is not a university, still less a mere *foundation* in a university, as in England. It resembles more nearly the preparatory schools, such as Eton and Rugby, in the British Isles, and the Gymnasia on the continent. Yet it differs in so many respects from any European institution, that it has sometimes been pronounced unique and peculiar to America. It has even been called an *Americanism.*

The place which the college holds among all the means of public instruction *at home,* is not less broadly and definitely marked. Quite distinct from the common school on the one hand, and from the professional seminary on the other, though sustaining important relations to both, the college is intended to lay a broad foundation in a thoroughly disciplined mind for all liberal culture, for all high attainments and achievements. Its principal aim is to develope and discipline the faculties, to call them into strenuous exercise, and impart to them a healthy tone, and train them for energetic, yet well balanced action; to give strength, beauty, and symmetry to the intellectual and moral powers: in a word, to *educate* the whole man. College is properly and pre-eminently an *educational* institution. And so thoroughly is this fact wrought into the consciousness of the community, that, in common parlance, an *educated* man is a man that has received a *college* education.

We have, indeed, had our self-educated men, and some of them have acted a very distinguished part in the history of our country; but as a general fact, *self*-educated men are *uneducated*, or *half*-educated at the best. They usually betray, if not a want of discipline and knowledge, at least a want of symmetry and completeness. They are not safe guides. They generally prove inadequate to trying emergencies; and the wisest and best men of this class have been among the foremost to recognize the necessity, and to aid in the advancement, of college education. The sagacious Franklin, with the good sense which was characteristic of him, drew up a project for the foundation of a college, in which he strongly recommended the study of the ancient languages for all the students, and insists on it for those who intend to engage in the learned professions.

"The Father of his Country" was a self-made man; but he felt the deficiency, and had recourse to a graduate of Columbia College (Alexander Hamilton) in the preparation of his most important State Papers. In his own writings, he often showed a want of that minute accuracy which belongs to a thoroughly educated man, so that President Sparks, with or without sufficient reason, felt under the necessity of sometimes correcting his language, when he edited his correspondence. And with the magnanimity and public spirit for which he was so remarkable, he bore testimony to the value of the literary advantages which he did not enjoy, by laying the foundation of a college in his native State, which honors, while it is honored by, the name of Washington.*

The distinguished orator and statesman of Kentucky was a self-taught man. But bitterly did he deplore his limited opportunities for early education. Especially in some of his severe conflicts with John Randolph on the floor of Congress, when taunted by him on the incorrect use of a word, Henry Clay would acknowledge, with tears, the disadvantage which he suffered, owing to the want of that liberal education which his antagonist had enjoyed.

The excellence of classical studies can hardly be better expressed than in the language of Franklin, in the project above mentioned: "When youth are told that the great men whose lives and actions they read in history spoke two of the best languages that ever were, the most expressive, copious, beautiful, and that the finest writings, the most correct compositions, the

* Washington College, Lexington, Va., was originally endowed by Washington with stock, which yields about $2500 annually.

most perfect productions of wit and wisdom, are in those languages which have endured for ages, and will endure while there are men; that no translation can do them justice, or give the pleasure found in reading the originals; that those languages contain all science; that one of them is become almost universal, being the language of learned men in all countries; and that to understand them is a distinguished ornament,—they may be made thereby desirous of learning those languages, and their industry sharpened in the acquisition of them."*

Besides classical studies (which are thus warmly and justly commended by Franklin), and the study of their own vernacular tongue, together with perhaps one or two of the other modern languages, young men in college apply themselves chiefly to the study of mathematics and physical and mental science, which, while they are admirably adapted to discipline the intellectual powers, are also designed to make the student acquainted with himself and the world he lives in; and so with that infinite Being—the highest of all the objects of knowledge—who is the Maker both of man and of the universe, and the original Author of all the science that pertains to both.

Their teachers also are expected to be men of thorough academical education, who have themselves travelled over all the road, and are able to point the way to others; who are themselves the embodiment of literature and science, and the patterns of that

* See Appendix to Sparks' Life of Franklin.

liberal culture which results from such studies; whose large acquaintance with the productions of men in every age, and with the works of God, has raised them above the low prejudices of time and place, carried them beyond the narrow bounds of what is merely local and temporary, and planted their feet in the vast open field of comprehensive wisdom, and on the solid basis of immutable truth; but who are yet *men*, with lively human sympathies, and fresh youthful feelings, —old heads on young shoulders; who will delight to take young men by the hand, and go over the whole field of knowledge with them, as if it were as new to them as it is to their pupils; and to work out with them anew, or rather set them to working out, each one for himself, under their guidance, the great problems of life and of the universe.

Aside from the direct influence of the best studies pursued under the best masters, students in college derive from their intercourse and communion with each other an invaluable discipline. Proceeding from all classes in society, and all parts of the country, bringing together their divers talents, tastes, habits and attainments, and acting and reacting upon one another by constant contact and collision during four years, and those among the most plastic and decisive years of their lives, they of necessity lose their idiosyncracies and provincial peculiarities and narrow prejudices in a broad, genial and liberal humanity; they rub off their sharp corners and projecting asperities, and are reduced to a more rounded symmetry and polished smoothness; they are brought down from their vanity and self-conceit, or brought up from their self-distrust and timidity, and each one finds the proper level of his own talents and attainments,—as shapeless opaque substances, dissolved in a fluid, assume forms of order and beauty ; as the very stones of the brook are worn by each other, and by the running water, to rotundity and polish.

Receiving students from all ranks and conditions, and sending them out again into all the professions, and the higher walks of life, the college, like the ocean, forms a connecting link among the fountains of influence, and a medium of communication and circulation between them and the streams. Not a section of the country, but pours into it larger or smaller tributary streams. Scarce a city or village, scarce a church or school, but receives back more or less abundant showers of refreshing influence. Planted by our fathers in the wilderness side by side with *republican liberty* and *primitive Christianity, college education* has grown with *their* growth, and strengthened with their strength, till now like three stately trees, of different form and kind, of separate life and organization, yet lending each to each mutual support, borrowing each from the others an added beauty, and each essential to the perfection, if not to the very existence, of the others ; they have struck their blended roots deep into every acre of our soil, and spread their interlaced branches wide over all the land, and men of every class and condition sit beneath their common shade, and eat in abundance of their diverse, yet wholesome fruit.

Harvard College was founded in 1638, only eighteen years after the first landing on Plymouth Rock; when Boston was a small village of not more than twenty or thirty houses, and when only twenty-five towns had begun to be settled in Massachusetts. It was one of the first things our Pilgrim Fathers thought of, and, as Cotton Mather well says, "it was the *best* thing they ever thought of." It was ever after cherished and provided for as a child, not only by appropriations from the Legislature, but by voluntary contributions of money or produce from the poorest of the people. Its constitution forms a part of the constitution of the State, and its life and history are inseparable from those of the Commonwealth for nearly two hundred years, during the greater part of which time it furnished nearly all the ministers and magistrates of old Massachusetts. It rendered the same service also to Connecticut, and the other New England colonies, till (feeling the necessity for a similar institution which should stand in the same near and intimate relation to their own organic life, to their own political and religious history) a few clergymen marked the *commencement* of a new *century* by founding Yale College in 1700, bringing a selection of books from their private libraries—forty volumes in all—saying, "These books we give for the founding of a college in Connecticut." William and Mary College, in Virginia, was established a few years earlier than Yale.

The *middle* of the eighteenth century was marked again by the establishment of the three oldest and most important institutions of the Middle States; the College of New Jersey, founded at Princeton, in 1746, and honored alike by its venerable line of presidents and its illustrious catalogue of graduates; Columbia College, founded at New York, in 1754, and then called King's College, though it educated something better than kings or courtiers; and the University of Pennsylvania, established one year later, in the city of Philadelphia. The middle of the *last half* of the same century was also characterized by the founding of Brown University in Rhode Island, Dartmouth College in New Hampshire, Dickinson College at Carlisle, in Pennsylvania; Hampden Sydney College in Virginia, Charleston College in Charleston, South Carolina; and the University of Georgia, at Athens: the first two established a little before, and the others just after, the war of the Revolution. The close of the century was signalized by the appearance, in rapid succession, of a whole galaxy of stars in our literary firmament; the Universities of Vermont and North Carolina in 1791, Williams College in 1793, Bowdoin in 1794, Union College in 1795, Middlebury in 1800, and Jefferson College and the Universities of Ohio and South Carolina in 1802.

A season of less activity ensued; a sort of lull between the political impulse communicated by the Revolution, and the new religious life which was imparted by missions and revivals in 1820; though, during this interval, Hamilton College was founded in 1812, and the University of Virginia in 1814. About the year 1820, commenced a new era in the history of colleges (of which we shall speak more particularly in another chapter), during which new colleges, from

Amherst in the East, to Iowa College in the far West, have risen upon the country with such rapidity,* and in such numbers, that specifications would be tedious, till we have already more than a hundred and twenty such institutions,—one or more in every State, under the instruction of six hundred teachers, and comprising an aggregate of more than ten thousand students.

Next to her political organization, we find each State looking out for a college, as if it was the light of her eyes, or the right arm of her strength. The colleges, like the churches of America, are for the most part separate from the organization of the State, and independent of its direct control. But they are for that reason none the less an essential part of our complex social, political and religious system. Nay, the people love their colleges, just as they do their churches, all the more because they are the offspring, not of government patronage, but of their own free-will offerings and voluntary sacrifices. Hence, the inhabitants of every State want a college, which they can call their own, as every body politic wants its own eyes or hands. Nay, every *section*, as well as every *sect*, wants its own college, that it may not only be within reach of their sons, but within sight of their own eyes, and more or less under their own control. This is doubtless carrying the matter to an excess. But even this has its good results. The *sight* of a college is one, and that no despicable means of educating the surrounding community. At least it shows that col-

Upon an average, one for every year of the present century.

leges are rooted in the hearts of the people. They have been assailed by demagogues and radical reformers; and there have been times when it seemed as if public sentiment would yield to the clamor. But true to the spirit of their fathers and the history of the country, the American people have always, ere long, returned to their first love, like the needle to the pole-star; and never was the system of collegiate education more strongly grounded in public confidence and affection than at this moment. It will be modified to suit the change of circumstances; it will be enlarged to meet the growing demands of the age; but it will not be abandoned,—it cannot be abolished. It has become a fixed fact. It is the settled policy of the country. The college is an essential element in our present social organization, even as it has been in all our past private and public history.

Remove the colleges, and you take down the whole fabric of our social, political and religious history. Extinguish the colleges, and you put out the eyes both of the church and of the State. Take away the colleges, and you leave education, politics and religion without competent guides; the school, the church and the State, all without a suitable head.

It is a prime characteristic of college education that it has to do with the leading minds of the community and the country; those who, by their talents and attainments, are destined to exert a controlling influence. Here is the hiding of its power. It teaches the teachers, and preaches to the preachers, and governs the governors. The ten thousand young men in

American colleges are but a small portion of the youth of America, but they will soon fill the larger part of the posts of honor and power in the church and in the State; and by their personal and official standing, as well as by the tongue, the pen and the press, they will exercise a commanding influence in society and in public affairs. Martin Luther's teacher at Eisenach never entered the school-room without taking off his hat, and bowing to his scholars. When his colleagues expressed their astonishment at his extreme condescension, he replied: "There are among these youth those whom God will one day raise to the rank of burgomasters, chancellors, doctors and magistrates." With far more reason might every man who enters or looks upon an American college, bare his head, and bow low before the assembled guides and rulers of the next generation.

Again (and this is the second secret of its power), the college takes these leading minds at an *age* when they may yet be moulded to truth and goodness, though they will soon be stiffened and hardened past any essential alteration; takes them in the *last period* of youth, and gives them the last touch of their education, properly so called, before their entrance upon manhood; receives them into its bosom to live as well as study under the care of professors, who stand in the double relation of teachers and parents, and exerts upon them the two-fold influence of the school and the family circle. Alexander the Great said: "Philip gave me life, Aristotle taught me how to live *well.*" We would not place the professor before the parent, or the college above the family, which is nature's own school, and in which the parent should be also the teacher, and not only give life, but guide to a life of wisdom and virtue. But next to home and the family circle, the college does most to shape the character of those who will so soon be the ruling spirits in every department of social and public life.

A third fact worthy of notice in regard to the influence of colleges is, that they are *permanent foundations*, and so give permanence to the institutions, whether of society, of government, or of education, which they control and supply.

The ministry cannot perpetuate itself. The magistracy cannot educate its own successors, and so perpetuate itself. The inferior departments of education cannot train their own men, and so sustain themselves. But let the college be well supported, and it will sustain, supply and perpetuate them all. It is at once the key-stone of the educational system, and the corner-stone of our civil and religious institutions. And for this very reason, it is liable to be depreciated by unobserving and unreflecting minds. The key-stone of the arch is too high up, too far removed from common observation, to be readily seen and appreciated. To a careless and superficial view, the arch might seem to be complete without it; but take it out, or never put it in, and the arch will not stand. The foundation stones of the temple lie too deep to be seen by common eyes, but the architect sees them buried deep in the ground, and no wise man will build a house without solid and enduring foundations; no

Christian will forget, that "except the Lord build the house, they labor in vain that build it;" no intelligent American citizen, who prays for any thing, can fail to pray that the foundations may be so laid in our colleges as not only themselves to last for many generations, but also to sustain and perpetuate all our republican and Christian institutions to the end of time.

CHAPTER V.

Colleges and Popular Education—Parts of one System—Must rise or fall together—Proved by Facts—By the Nature of the Case—Men of Collegiate Discipline the best Teachers in any School—Needed to train Teachers of Common Schools—To prepare Text-books—To direct Popular Education—Engineers—Light-houses and Observatories—Early Settlers of Massachusetts—Free Colleges—Revivals in Common Schools taught by College Students—The Common School Question to be settled in the Colleges—The Jesuits—A Teaching Order—Austria—Poland—America—Must be met with their own Weapons.

THE intimate and essential relation which subsists between colleges and the whole scheme of popular education, is not well understood; still less is it duly appreciated. Ignorant men have even indulged a suspicion that there is a necessary antagonism between the education of the few in colleges and the education of the masses in common schools; and designing demagogues have not been slow to foster this popular prejudice, and take advantage of it for their own selfish aggrandizement. But the whole history of education in our country shows, that so far from being antagonistic to each other, colleges and common schools form different and essential parts of one and the same great system, which must live or die, rise or fall, flourish or decay together. Facts prove that where colleges are best sustained, there common schools are most fostered ; that the States and sections where the standard of collegiate education is most elevated, are the very States and sections where the standard of teachers and pupils in the common schools is the highest ; that the success and usefulness of common schools is exactly proportioned to the popularity and prosperity of colleges, and that whatever is done for or against the one is sure to react with equal force and with similar results upon the other.

In the nature of things, the facts could not well be otherwise. Education, as well as every other *living* thing, must have a *head,* as well as hands and feet. Common schools and academies, select schools and high schools, and all the lower seminaries, must have not only scholars, but teachers, and committees, and guardians, and examiners, and text-books, and apparatus, and all suitable means and appliances, not only to keep them up to their present standard, but to carry them forward in a constant progress towards perfection. And the men who are to do all this must be thoroughly educated men, disciplined in all their faculties, and masters of all literature and science ; well acquainted with their own minds, and the minds of others, as well as with the structure of the human body and the constitution of the universe.

So far reaching and universal are the relations of things, that no one thing can be fully known without a knowledge of a multitude of other things. Hence, in order to teach any thing to the best advantage, the teacher needs to know not merely that particular thing, but every thing else to which it stands related. The best method of teaching a child his alphabet is a question involving profound principles of philology, as well as mental philosophy. None but a profound scholar and philosopher is qualified to make a spelling-book. Webster studied and improved on his spelling-book, after he had finished the best dictionary of the English language, and had placed himself in the very foremost rank of English philologists. A good reading-book can be prepared only by a man of correct taste, wide acquaintance with literature and finished classical education. No man can make a good English grammar who knows only the English language. The best English grammars, not to say all the improvements in the method of teaching English grammar, have been made by profound classical scholars, availing themselves, too, of the labors of still more learned men, still more profoundly versed in comparative philology. The best text-books in the natural sciences for the use of schools and academies have been prepared by the professors and teachers of natural science in college; and well they may have been, for they require an extensive acquaintance with both natural and mental philosophy.

The same principles apply to teachers, not less than authors of text-books. Other things being equal, the more a man knows of every thing, the better he can teach any thing; and the more thorough and complete the discipline of his own mind, the better he can impart even a little discipline to the mind of another. A well educated man will give the best education to a child. A gentleman of high classical discipline and attainments is the best teacher of young ladies in the solid branches. And a genuine scholar, philosopher, sage, who has not lost his common sense and his sympathy with the young,—old in wisdom, but young in feeling and affection,—would be the best teacher of any, even the simplest and humblest branch of learning.

We do not, indeed, expect all the teachers in our common schools to be men of college education, or even women of equivalent attainments; but we do affirm that, other things being equal, the more they know the better they will teach in any sphere; and that in proportion as the teachers in our common schools advance towards the standard of a full collegiate education, common schools themselves will advance in substantial excellence and usefulness. And they who are to sit in judgment on both teachers and text-books, they who are to give shape and direction to the public schools of a town, of a State, of a nation, *must* be men of thoroughly disciplined minds and extensive attainments, who can look out over the whole field of knowledge, and see every thing, not only in its immediate bearings, but in its ultimate tendencies and results.

The friends of common schools jealous of colleges! It is most irrational and absurd; nay, it is suicidal. As well might the travelling public be jealous of scientific schools for the education of engineers! The system of *public schools* must be under the control of well trained, skilful and faithful engineers, or the road will be wrongly laid and badly constructed, and the train will be perpetually running off the track. As well might common sailors look with a suspicious eye upon the astronomical observatories that adorn our cities, or the light-houses that line our coasts. Our gallant *public school marine* must have its observatories and its light-houses, or, bravely as it has sailed out of port, it will ere long encounter head-winds and unforeseen currents, and be dashed, an utter wreck, on an unknown shore; or, what is scarcely less deplorable, drift helmless and helpless, without compass, chart or nautical almanac, at the mercy of the winds and waves.

The entire system of education, as it has come down to us from a wise and godly ancestry, is one organic body, having a head as well as a trunk and lower members, animated from head to foot with the same life, and pervaded from the heart to the extremities by the same vital energies. The first literary institution which the early settlers of Massachusetts founded higher than *common schools* was a *college.* Eleven years after, it was ordered by the General Court, that "when any town shall increase to the number of one hundred families, they shall set up a *grammar school,* the master thereof being able to instruct youth so far as they may be fitted for the *university.*" Thus, within thirty years after the landing of the Pilgrims, they had laid the foundations of our entire educational system, with its three grades of schools, essentially as they now exist. And they nurtured and cherished the whole system as a whole, watching and caring for it in every part; and their *sons*, if they would have it live and thrive, must foster it with the same impartial and comprehensive wisdom.

The State should extend not its direct governmental control, but its sustaining and fostering hand, alike to the higher and the lower seminaries, and give us not only free common and high schools, but free academies and colleges, where rich and poor shall meet together at "the upper and the nether springs," and mutually know and educate each other, with no aristocracy but that of talent and learning; no distinctions of rank and standing, but those of wisdom and goodness.

The Church, through her ministers and members, should lend a helping hand at every stage of the process, and not only extend to it the patronage of her sons and daughters (none too *rich* to patronise the *common schools*, and none too *poor* to be represented in the *colleges*), but bestow on it also the richer blessing of her prayers, and infuse into it the purifying and life-giving influence of her principles and spirit. The providence of God has given her in a great measure the control of the colleges of our land, and thus (if she did but know it) the indirect control of academies and common schools. The religious influence which college students exert, as *teachers* of common schools, *during* their *college course*, is beyond calculation. The greater part of those who teach in this way are young men of devoted piety, who avail themselves of this as the only practicable method of realizing the fondest desire of their hearts, which is to be educated for the Christian ministry. How many precious revivals of religion have originated in the faithful labors of such teachers in common schools, and have spread, not only through the school, but through the whole community! How many more would thus originate if all who go forth from our colleges, from year to year, to spend a term in the instruction of common schools, were imbued with the full *spirit* of revivals, of the gospel ministry, and of Christian missions! And if all our educated men who have any thing to do with common schools, were men who reverence the Bible, and love and obey its sacred truths, how much could they do, directly or indirectly, to leaven with the same holy sentiments the entire rising generation! It is in the *colleges*, after all, that the common school question, with all its momentous bearings on the church and the State, is to be mainly decided. Let then those who love the church and the State,—let those who seek the good of the rising generation, pray that all the young men in our colleges may be imbued with the truth of God and the love of Christ, and what the church cannot do directly (owing to the popular jealousy of sectarianism, and of the union of church and State), these young men will do for her; they will leaven every department of public and private education, not with the creeds and formularies of a sect, but with the vital spirit of a common Protestant Christianity.

It was in just this way that those world-renowned educators and conquerors, the Jesuits, recovered the larger part of Europe to the papacy, when it seemed lost for ever. They seized upon the higher departments of education, both private and public, and from these fountains, whether in universities or courts, or the families of the great, their influence flowed naturally and necessarily down through the inferior schools and the lower classes, till at length it pervaded all the channels of thought and feeling and action. At some periods of their history, the Jesuits have had under their control nearly six hundred colleges, scattered from China to the British Isles, through almost every nation on the globe. This most energetic and effective,—this almost omnipresent and all-powerful order, has ever been, not so much a preaching or a priestly, as a *teaching* order; an order of professors and governors, and scholars and teachers, who have made it their business to *educate* the leading minds, and through them to guide and govern communities and nations. Austria herself was at one time essentially Protestant. "Not one in thirty of the population adhered to papacy, and, for nearly a generation, scarcely a man was found to enter the Romish priesthood." But the Jesuits went forth; they marched directly to the fountains; "they obtained a controlling influence in the universities, and in a single generation Austria was lost to the Reformation, and regained to the papal hierarchy." *

Very similar is the history of the Reformation in Poland. In the sixteenth century, the Polish Diet was a Protestant body, and exerted its influence for

* Ranke's History of the Popes, as cited by Prof. Sturtevant before the West. Coll. Soc.

the protection of persecuted Protestants in other countries. Luther's works were printed at Cracow; and in other cities of Poland, presses in great numbers were employed in printing Protestant books, which could not be printed elsewhere. But in an evil hour, a Protestant king, chosen by a Protestant Diet, appointed a Jesuit minister of public instruction. He filled the professors' chairs in the universities and higher seminaries with the members of his own order. The scale was soon turned, and the doctrines of the Reformation never again recovered the ascendency.

"*Fas est et ab hoste doceri.*" We may well learn a lesson of worldly wisdom from these consummate masters. And the lesson which their history teaches is this: educate the leading minds, and the rest will be sure to follow in their train; get possession of the colleges, and you can control popular education and public opinion as you will. It is these same Jesuits, armed with the same policy, with whom the Protestant Christians of America have to contend for the mastery of the New World. And the only way to conquer them is to meet them with their own weapons, to anticipate and surpass them in their own mode of warfare; to seize upon the prominent points, and establish the higher seminaries, and educate the controlling spirits of the community. Allow *them* to secure the colleges, male and female, and form the leading minds of a single generation, and they will not only appropriate the public-school fund to the support of their own schools, and gather into them the children of Protestant families, but they will gradually insinuate their teachers into Protestant schools and Protestant families; and then the victory will be theirs. And when the *Jesuits* conquer and govern America, it will be *America* no longer. With the truth, she will have lost her liberty and her glory for ever.

CHAPTER VI.

Colleges and the Literature of the Country, or the Power of the Pen and the Press—Contributions of the Officers to Literature and Science—The Edwardses, Davies, Dwight, &c.—Libraries and Lecture-rooms the homes of Men of Letters—The Minds of Students fruitful in new and grand Ideas—Bacon, Milton—Theological Literature of the Puritans the Fruit of Classical Scholarship—Bates, Howe, Owen, Cudworth—English Science and Philosophy—Newton—British Poets and Essayists—French Literature and Port Royal—The Press divides with the Pulpit the Power over the Public Mind—Educated Men alone can give this Power a right Direction—Oxford Tracts—Infidel Literature—Temperance, Liberty and Humanity.

THE obligations of literature and science to our colleges are too obvious to require extended remark. Literature and science are, so to speak, at once the labor and the wages, the seed and the harvest, the capital stock and the dividend, of these institutions.

The officers, while they teach others, must study themselves. And not content with the attainments and discoveries of their predecessors, they are ambitious to enlarge the boundaries of human knowledge. Not confining their view to their immediate pupils, they labor for the diffusion of learning through the community. The libraries and the lecture-rooms of the professors are so many centres of attraction, which draw in men of leisure and taste, who make the college their home, and literature their profession. To specify the contributions that have been made by the presidents and fellows, the professors and resident graduates in the colleges and universities of Europe, or even of America, during the present and the previous century, were to enumerate no small portion of the books that have appeared, especially in the more profound and useful branches—were to write in no small measure the history of these branches during this period.

The students, too, do not all converse with learned men, and breathe the atmosphere of libraries and books four years, to no purpose. The natural excitability of youth, the fermentation produced by bringing together so many youthful minds, the high excitement resulting in these minds from the rapid influx of new and grand ideas,—all conspire to render the soil and the very atmosphere of a college quickening and prolific, far beyond the knowledge or the conception of those who are not acquainted with the facts. Not a few of those great works which have revolutionized the opinions, and changed the history of mankind, have been *projected by university students.* During the four years which Lord Bacon spent in the university of Cambridge, he had already formed a distinct idea of the defects of the Aristotelian system of philosophy, and conceived the outline of that gigantic plan for "the Instauration of the Sciences," which has rendered his name immortal, and converted philosophy from a barren wilderness into a fruitful field. Such novel and noble ideas, Mr. Hallam observes, "are most congenial to the sanguine spirit of youth, and to its ignorance of the extent of labor it undertakes;" and the university furnishes just the stimulus and just the nutriment that are needed to excite and sustain the youthful energies in such undertakings.

Milton remained in the university for only a part of the regular course, and left it without much partiality for its methods of study and discipline. Yet he forged in the university the very arms which he turned against it; and there, in a thoroughly disciplined mind, and highly cultivated taste, as well as abundant classical learning, he laid the foundation of his great works. The "Paradise Lost" is hung all over with the trophies of classical scholarship, and affords a splendid illustration of the use which original genius and puritanical piety can make of a complete academic education. The theological literature of the Puritans generally, and, indeed, all the theological literature of that age,—the age of Hooker and Barrow and Taylor, of Bates and Howe, and Owen and Cudworth,—was the product of minds thoroughly trained in the universities, and furnishes a bright example of the value of classical scholarship, sanctified and consecrated to the service of religion. The theological writers of our own country, who have so honored the country in the eyes of the world, have been men who learned in college to unite the study of human learning with the wisdom which cometh down from above. Chauncey, Mather, the two Edwardses, Dwight, Davies, Witherspoon, Appleton, and others, whom we might name, were not only alumni, but presidents of American colleges.

The fathers of English science and philosophy, from Bacon and Newton and Locke, to Stewart and Whewell and Buckland; from the Novum Organum and the Principia to the Bridgewater Treatises, and the History of the Inductive Sciences,—have spent years, and many of them lived and died, at the universities. "Newton was nurtured in academic discipline, a fellow in Trinity College, Cambridge, and a professor of mathematics. He passed fifteen years of his life in the cloisters of a college, and solved the problem of the universe from a turret over Trinity gateway." *

The British essayists, and even the novelists, for the most part, and still more generally the poets of Great Britain, wandered in their youth on the banks of the Cam and the Isis, and ever after drew water from those classic streams. Not to indulge in further specifications, the greater part, and by far the better part, of English, including American literature, has been the fruit directly or indirectly of college labors and studies, of tastes, habits and acquirements formed in the university. Some of the finest verses of Racine were meditated while, a boy at school, he wandered in the woods of Port Royal. The Letters and the Thoughts of Pascal, pregnant with human genius and divine wisdom, were composed in the same sacred retreat.

Now and then a Shakspeare has arisen with such transcendent genius as to supersede the necessity of the ordinary training; who has acquired the needful discipline and resources by observation and reflection, and sent out his plays to the world boasting that he "never blotted a line." But his best friend, and most ardent admirer, has been constrained to respond:

* Mr. Everett on behalf of the Colleges of Massachusetts.

"Would God, he had blotted a thousand." Some of the most impure and lawless effusions of the poetic and romantic muse have proceeded from men who, like Byron and Shelley, could not brook the restraints of college law, or had no relish for the pursuits of college life, and were even expelled from the university. A still lower and baser class of books, the yellow-covered literature of the day, savors rather of the bar-room, the brothel and the prison, than the university. The schools are all guiltless of their sins. Their authors never saw the inside of a college.

The question, who shall furnish the country with reading, with books and pamphlets, and magazines, with quarterlies and monthlies, and weeklies and dailies, is a question of incalculable moment. It is almost equivalent to the question, what shall be the prevailing thoughts and sentiments, character and spirit of the people. In an age and country like ours, where every body reads, able and eloquent writers form almost the atmosphere in which the whole community live and move and have their being. The pulpit was once the throne whence the people derived, *ex cathedra*, their doctrines and duties. The press is now the oracle of multitudes who seldom or never hear the preacher's voice, and it divides the sovereignty with the pulpit over the minds of church-goers and Christians. Hoe's rotary press will now throw off an amount of work in an hour which a week could not accomplish with the common hand-press. While the mechanical efficiency of the press has thus been magnified a hundredfold, its moral power has been increasing in the same astonishing ratio. Now the question, who shall wield this mighty moral engine (a question which is to decide in a great measure the character and destiny of the present and coming generations for time and eternity), is itself to be decided, to a great extent, in the colleges.

Say what you will of a growing distance between colleges and the public mind ; admit all that can be said of the increasing influence of a new class of popular writers, who have never seen the inside of a college, and who have got their education in the streets and market-places of the city, if not even in worse places than these ; concede all on this point that the truth will justify, still the educated men of the country, if sufficiently numerous, and able, and well educated, can, and will, control the literature of the country. At all events, if they cannot control it, and, with the blessing of God, give it a right direction, no human power can. We are shut up to this resource. This is our only hope. If we would preserve or cherish a literature truthful, earnest and pure, that shall bless the present generation, and honor the country in the eyes of the world in future ages, we must make pure, and keep pure, the colleges, as the only fountains from which such a literature can flow.

Let the colleges of our land be given up to the sole inspiration of pagan muses, and a corrupting and degrading heathen literature will dishonor and defile the land. Let Jesuitism and Popery, open or disguised, establish their reign in the universities, and the Oxford Tracts, with their effete superstitions and defunct ceremonials and Jesuitical ethics, will overspread the country, like the flies and the locusts of Egypt. Again, let skepticism, whether in the guise of soaring transcendentalism, or in the form of grovelling infidelity, seat itself in the professors' chairs, and a darkness, that can be felt, damp, chilly and penetrating, will settle down upon us, or a plague, loathsome as that of the frogs, will come into our houses and to our very hearths. If the moral atmosphere of the college be pure, and the standard of piety high,—if truth and temperance, justice, liberty and humanity be the reigning ideas of the institution, the young men who go forth from it will, for the most part, range themselves on the right side in the great conflict of principles that is now going on, and their pens will fight battles and win triumphs more glorious than were ever won by the sword. If, on the other hand, error and intemperance, injustice and oppression, be suffered to reign and riot in these halls of learning, the same spirits of darkness will fly abroad over the community, armed with the pen and the press, making havoc with the bodies and the souls of men, and revelling in the sighs and tears, and blood of oppressed humanity.

CHAPTER VII.

Colleges in their relation to the Business of Life and the Affairs of State—The intrinsic Value of Educated Men—Knowledge is Power—Intelligence and Virtue the Wealth of the Community—Speculative and Scientific Men the Creators of Material Wealth—Authors of Useful Inventions and Discoveries—Chemistry and Agriculture and Manufactures—Science and the Steamship, the Rail-car and the Magnetic Telegraph—Bacon, Newton and Locke—Watt and Fulton—Professor Morse—No Progress without Science—Science saves Time and misdirected Effort—Most useful in an enterprising Age—Sociology the study of our Age—Our Country's Mission to perfect and apply the Science—English Statesmen trained in the Universities—The Founders of our Republic, Hamilton, Madison, Jay, Jefferson—Early Magistrates of New England Graduates of Harvard, Yale, Nassau Hall and Columbia Colleges—University Students Revolutionary in Despotisms, and Conservative in England and America—Influence of Colleges at once Conservative and Progressive, Classical and Christian—Friendly to the Union, but hostile to perpetual Annexation, Manifest Destiny, &c.—These Popular Heresies can be corrected only by the Blessing of God on our Colleges.

WHAT have colleges to do with politics and the business of life? What possible connection is there between the brown studies of the cloister and the noise and stir of the work-a-day world, which is the abode of ordinary men, women and children? Is there not a natural and necessary antagonism between the speculative theories of the scholar and the practical demands of business, which has passed into a proverb, and rendered the very names of scholar and scholastic a by-word—a synonym with the grossest ignorance and incapacity in the common affairs of every-day life? In one word, of what use are colleges in an age and country so practical and enterprising as ours?

We might ask, if literature and science have no *intrinsic* value,—if wisdom and goodness are not of themselves useful,—if the very presence of educated men is not a blessing to the community,—if they do not, by their example and influence, promote intelligence, good order and good morals,—and if these are not the true wealth and power of any people? If knowledge is power, and virtue is wealth, then are not educated Christian men among the most productive classes in society?

But we will not insist on this view. We choose rather to meet the question, just as it is asked, with reference to mere material wealth, and the lowest practical utility. Is there, then, a natural antagonism between theory and practice? between science and art? between study and action? between the past and the future? Is not theory rather the mother of practical wisdom, and science the fountain of improvement in the arts? and study the very basis of the most effective action? and the past the nursery and school,—nay, the parent and teacher of the future? The men who, in every age, have been on the largest scale practical and useful men,—those who have been the creators of material wealth and prosperity,—have been men of science and speculation. They may not have been understood or appreciated in their own day, but after ages have looked back to them as the men whose discoveries and inventions have revolutionized business, politics, society, and the whole history of mankind. Alchemy, in the middle ages, gave birth to chemistry; and chemistry is now the teacher of agriculture and manufactures. Science was born in the cloister, and nursed in the laboratory and cabinet; but now she drives the steamship and rail-car, and carries the news from one extremity of the land to the other with the speed of the lightning. Now she is the counsellor of kings and commanders, the prime minister of princely merchants, the guiding agent, and yet the obedient servant of manufacturers; the fairy-like favorite of those most independent of all lords,—the lords of the soil; and the presiding genius in every department of business.

Who have ever contributed more largely to the means and materials of human prosperity and progress than those sons of the English universities, Bacon, Newton, and Locke? Watt and Fulton, though not themselves men of academical education, associated familiarly with such men, and derived from them the principles of science which they applied in the development of the steam-engine and steam navigation. Professor Morse, the inventor of the electric telegraph, was not only a college graduate and professor, but made his great experiments within the walls of a university. The farmer, who would know how to multiply his crops without increasing the number of his acres, has only to inquire of Professor Liebig in his laboratory; and the navigator, who would double the number of his voyages in a given time, and so double his profits, without adding to his expenses, need but consult Lieutenant Maury in his study.

Two centuries ago, there might have been some plausibility in the charge, that science was unpractical and unfruitful; though even then she was the author of all the progress that was made; even then she was slowly elaborating those elements and processes which are now most fruitful in practical results. But in this nineteenth century, when every department of life is teeming with the fruits of science in its infinitely various applications, such a complaint is preposterous. It is, however, no uncommon thing for men to forget their benefactors in the very enjoyment of their benefactions; to feel quite independent of the fountain, because of the very richness and copiousness of the draughts which they drink from the stream. Thus infidelity "abstracts the coin of heaven,"—the truths of revelation, "and stamps them with the image and superscription of reason." And thus, too, the excessive utilitarianism of our age denies her obligations to literary and scientific institutions, while, at the same time, she is rioting in the wealth and luxury which literature and science are pouring into her lap. Let the fountain be dried up, and they would soon, though too late, discover and deplore their error. Cut off business from science, and there is an end of progress; and where progress ends, a retrograde movement almost certainly begins. Separate the future from the past, and it settles down into a tame, dull, stationary present; nay, it soon sinks back into a dark, cold, dead and dismal past, in which there is no life, and from which there is no resurrection. The men who are most thoroughly masters of all past attainments, are, of all men, the best prepared, and the most likely, with equal original genius, to strike out new and useful inventions. And the men of the greatest original and inventive genius, of all men, most *need* the wisdom of past ages, and the knowledge of the present, to guard them against a useless waste of their powers. What an untold amount of time and money, of ingenuity and effort, have such men wasted on perpetual motion, "squaring the circle," and the like insoluble problems, the impossibility of which every college student knows to a demonstration? Who can calculate the contributions which they would have added to the sum total of the means of human progress and happiness, if their genius had been guided by sound science; for such men, of all others, are most capable of turning all knowledge to a good practical account. An inventive, enterprising, progressive age and nation, of all others, most requires, and can profit most, by the knowledge of antiquity, and the discipline of classical studies. A utilitarian age and nation should be the last to discard or undervalue colleges, since they furnish at once the antidote to excessive utilitarianism, and the guide to true utility. They are at once the repositories of ancient wisdom, and the laboratories of modern science. The votaries of either must go on pilgrimage to the same shrine; and if in the pursuit of the one, they become enamored of the other also, and go away with a more impartial and liberal culture than they sought, the result will be happy for themselves and for the country.

What we have said of business, applies with double emphasis to politics, or the art of government. Government, or politics, or, to use a still more generic term, *sociology*, is just beginning to assume the form of a science second in difficulty, dignity and importance, only to that of theology. A wide observation of facts, and a profound study of principles alone, can bring it to perfection ; these alone can prevent it from being perverted into a crude mass of speculative notions and popular caprices, which, undergoing the process of fermentation and spontaneous combustion, may wrap the world in the flames of a vast political and social conflagration, or, enveloping the nations in poisonous gases and mephitic vapors, may involve them in a slower, but not less dreadful destruction. History and philosophy are the natural and necessary handmaids of this new science ; the torch-bearers of her progress, to shed on her adventurous and difficult path all the light they can gather from ransacking the ages and nations that are past, on the one hand, and, on the other, all that they can bring up from the deep recesses of human nature. Men of extensive knowledge and deep thought are needful to develope and mature the science. And then men of thoroughly disciplined minds and comprehensive views, and well-balanced character, are needed to apply the science to the actual perfecting of society and government. This is the great work of our age, and it is especially the mission, —the *political* mission, of our country.

The political philosophers and practical statesmen of such an age and such a country, cannot dispense with the experience of the past, and the wisdom of antiquity. Still less can they dispense with the personal discipline and mental balance, the moderation and self-control, which are usually the result only of a thorough education. England has set a noble exam ple in this regard. The eminent statesmen who have guided her safely through the many terrible storms of her long voyage, and brought her so near to the haven of a well-regulated liberty, imbibed the spirit of freedom and moderation from the study of the ancient republics in the universities. The ablest of these statesmen were, in their youth, the foremost scholars in the universities. "Take the Cambridge calendar," says Macaulay, in one of his speeches in Parliament,—"take the Cambridge calendar, or take the Oxford calendar, for two hundred years ; look at the church, the parliament, or the bar, and it has always been the case that the men who were first in the competition of the schools, have been the first in the competition of life."

The founders of our own republic, too, astonished the world by their boldness, and yet by their wisdom, because, though born and bred in this Western wilderness, they evinced in their writings so perfect an acquaintance with the political history and philosophy of ancient times. The Federalist, and the State papers of that day generally, are models in their kind, and present a standing illustration of the use which republican statesmen can make of the experience of ancient nations, even while they take the longest strides in improving the frame of civil government. The writers of the Federalist, who also bore a prominent part in framing the Constitution of the United States —Hamilton, Madison and Jay—were alumni of Columbia College, and the College of New Jersey. The author of the Declaration of Independence was a member of Hampden Sydney College, and its advocate on the floor of Congress was a graduate of Harvard University. The multitudes from this and other lands who go on pilgrimage to the tomb at Monticello, read there the inscription: "Thomas Jefferson, Author of the Declaration of Independence, and Founder of the University of Virginia." The inscription was penned by himself, and placed there by his own direction. He knew that knowledge is the handmaid of Liberty, and he wished to be remembered not only among the fathers of republics, but among the founders of universities.

The Pilgrim Fathers of New England deemed an educated magistracy next to, and in connection with, an educated ministry, of indispensable necessity to the well-being of the church and the state; and it was with this twofold view, that they established Harvard University at the very commencement of their colonial history, building it on the borders of that unbroken wilderness which still covered the New World. In the early history of the colonies, the magistrates and ministers were, for the most part, ripe scholars from the English universities, especially Cambridge, and they could not feel that their social and political organization was complete, till *New* England also had its *university at Cambridge.*

The civil and political history of New England and the Middle States for half a century before and after the Revolution, may almost be read in the large capitals which distinguish the governors and judges, the senators and representatives in Congress, on the catalogues of Harvard, Yale, Nassau Hall and Columbia Colleges. Let those who doubt the practical utility of colleges, or the political capacity of college-educated men, examine these catalogues. We should like to put those demagogues, who would fain create a prejudice against colleges in the public mind, to the study of those triennials (if, indeed, they are capable of mastering the easy Latin in which they are composed). Few books would teach them sounder doctrines; few furnish them brighter examples. Yale College has educated four of the signers of the Declaration of Independence, three members of the Convention for framing the Constitution of the United States, one Vice-President, four Judges of the Supreme Court of the United States, seven members of the Cabinet, thirty-nine United States Senators, one hundred and thirty-nine Representatives in Congress, four Foreign Ministers, twenty-two Governors, eighteen Lieutenant-Governors, and eighty Judges of the Supreme Court in different States; thirteen Presidents of Medical Societies, thirty-six Presidents of Colleges, and one hundred and five Professors. The College of New Jersey has furnished one President, two Vice-Presidents, four Judges of the Supreme Court of the United States, fifteen Judges of Supreme Courts in the several States, twenty Governors of States, six members of the Cabinet at Washington, and one hundred and twenty members of Congress. Harvard College has graduated two Presidents of the United States, one Vice-President, and Governors, Lieutenant-Governors, Secretaries, &c., &c., too numerous to mention. Of the thirty-five thousand graduates* that have been sent out from American Colleges, nearly two hundred have been Governors, more than five hundred Representatives in Congress, one hundred and thirty Senators of the United States, and nearly four hundred Judges of Supreme Courts.

Self-taught men have filled at times the highest places in our national and State governments; and this fact marks at once the strict equality and the elevating tendency of our political system. But the men who have given *shape* and *character* to our institutions have been, to a very great extent, men of liberal education. Classical studies are peculiarly fitted to form republican statesmen. They exert at once a stimulating and a moderating, an emancipating and a conservative influence. Hence the remarkable, and, at first view, apparently inexplicable fact, that on the European continent the members of the universities are generally revolutionary and republican in their tendencies,† while in England and America, where a large measure of freedom already exists, they are usually conservative,—very seldom radical in their politics. Classical literature, and, indeed, the living and breathing literature of the world,—the literature which men will not let die,—is all saturated with the spirit of liberty. It is, in no small measure, the undying

* This calculation was made in 1846. The *number* has of course greatly increased since, but the *proportion* remains about the same.

† See, for example, Flagg's Venice, on the part which the professors and students of the universities took in the Revolutions of 1848.

voice of the heroes and martyrs of freedom and humanity, sounding along down the ages of the past, and pouring its swelling and stirring notes into the ear of the present. But while this voice stirs the souls of youthful statesmen to their lowest depths, it also warns and awes, softens and subdues them. While it invites and commands them to strike for liberty and humanity,—strike at all wrong and oppression, and abuse of power, it also bids them beware of violence and excess as the bane of free States.

With this exciting, and, at the same time, restraining influence of the ancient classics, the divine teachings of the Bible harmonize, building the just and equal rights of all mankind upon the firm foundation of the immutable law of God, and making them free indeed, with the largest liberty, yet forbidding them by the most sacred sanctions to use their liberty as a cloak of licentiousness. If all the youth, who are to be the rulers and guides of our country in the next generation, could but be brought under such an influence, democratic, yet obedient to law, progressive, yet conservative, classical, and at the same time Christian, then might we live and die in the confident assurance that our liberties would be safe, our institutions perpetual. The mere bringing together of so many of the future statesmen and lawgivers of our country from different sections, and educating them together, tends to perpetuate the Union. Statesmen who have been *educated*, and educated *together* in the same institutions and the same classes, will be slow to rend asunder a Union, which is cemented by so many social ties and sacred recollections, as well as so many bonds of common interest. Christian scholars are not likely to be the men who will pamper the national pride and ambition on the gross and fatal, though popular fallacies, of military glory, "manifest destiny," and "our country right or wrong," till the moral sense of the people is blinded, and their unbounded appetite can be sated only by universal annexation. If this national appetite, which grows with what it feeds upon, is ever to be restrained,—if these dangerous political heresies are ever to be corrected,—it must be done at those fountains of public instruction, where our youthful politicians imbibe the political and moral sentiments that govern their lives, and shape the destinies of the country; and that, as we believe, in answer to the prayers of those who love at once their country and their God. And if we ever despair of the republic, it is only *when*, and *because*, we see how little prayer is offered, and with how little reliance on its efficacy, even by Christian patriots, for those who *are*, and those who are soon to *be*, the rulers of this great nation.

CHAPTER VIII.

Colleges and the Churches—Remark of Dr. Dwight—Himself a Demonstration of its Truth—Schools and Colleges owe their Origin to the Church—Christianity friendly to Learning—Paul a distinguished Scholar—Theological Schools at Jerusalem, Alexandria, &c.—Religious Origin of European Universities—Oxford, Cambridge, &c.—Of American Colleges, Harvard, Yale, &c.—Infidelity and State Policy unsuccessful in their attempts to build Colleges—Universities of Virginia and South Carolina—Girard College—Wonderful success of the Voluntary Principle and the Christian Spirit in such Enterprises—What Colleges have done in return for the Church—Indirectly through Christian Schools—A Christian Press—Christian Rulers and Professional Men—Directly in an Educated Ministry—Proportion of Ministers to whole Number of Graduates in different Colleges at different times—The Reformation sprung from the Universities—Methodism—Missions—Revivals—The Oxford Heresy—The Unitarian Defection—The Fountain and the Stream.

Dr. Dwight is said to have remarked to a clerical friend, that *the man who would show to common minds the connection between colleges and the interests of the church, would be a benefactor to his species.* It were sufficient to point to Dr. Dwight himself in proof of this connection. Behold in *himself*, we might well respond, the very demonstration which he asked. Behold it in his own life and writings, which present so fine a model of the Christian scholar and theological writer, popularizing and vitalizing theology, corroborating revelation by the light of nature and human reason, illustrating the truth of God by the literature and science, and history of men; and thus commanding for it the assent and obedience of the loftiest intellects, while, at the same time, he commended it to the understanding and affections of the humblest minds! Behold it in his commanding personal and official influence over his pupils, whereby he convinced the skeptical, and reclaimed the vicious, and quickened the dull, and elevated the grovelling; whereby he transformed the creed and the conduct, the morals and the religion, of Yale College, making it a school of Christ instead of a school of infidelity,—and wherein, though dead, he yet liveth, and speaketh with mighty power to the children and the children's children of those who enjoyed his instructions. If one president of one college could accomplish so much for "the interests of the church," what might not be done by all the officers of all the colleges of America, if they were clothed with his spirit and power!

But let us look a little more extensively into the origin and history of colleges, that we may see what has actually been their relation to the interests of the church.

Schools and colleges, wherever they exist, almost without exception, owe their origin to the church. Christianity is, in its very nature, friendly to learning. It is a religion not of forms and of ceremonies, but of the mind and heart. It saves men, not by outward means and appliances, but by the inward workings of the truth and the Spirit of God in their souls. Knowledge is, therefore, essential to holiness and salvation. Its ministry is a teaching and preaching ministry, not a mere officiating and manipulating priesthood. Its sacred books contain not only the most stirring truths, and the most commanding motives, but the choicest specimens of history, poetry and philosophy, the world has ever seen; and those, too, originally communicated in a foreign language, and for this reason, as well as many others, requiring prolonged study and extensive knowledge, in order to their full understanding and appreciation. Christianity produces an inquiring, observing, thinking and intelligent laity. It demands a reading, studying, reflecting and learned ministry.

The first ministers of the gospel were taught immediately by Christ, and were, moreover, constantly under the especial divine teaching of the Holy Spirit. They, therefore, stood in little need of human learning. Yet one of the apostles, and one who exceeded all the others in his labors and usefulness, was taught in the best Jewish and Gentile schools of Jerusalem and Tarsus. And no sooner were the miraculous gifts, which signalized the first establishment of Christianity, withdrawn, than the churches began to found colleges and theological schools at Jerusalem and Alexandria, and the other principal cities, for the especial purpose of raising up a pious and learned ministry, who should be able not only to preach the truth to its friends, but also to defend it from the assaults of its adversaries. And though, during the middle ages, learning every where suffered a disastrous eclipse, yet what light there was, shone from the schools in the monasteries, which were established by such enlightened and pious princes as Charlemagne and Alfred, chiefly for the elevation of the clergy, and which gradually grew up into universities. As this eclipse passed off slowly, and universities began to appear in Italy, in France, in England, they were established and fostered by the church, and chiefly for the better education of the clergy. Oxford and Cambridge were founded, and in the course of time enriched with princely endowments for this express purpose. Zeal for religion conspired with love of learning, and college after college was added to those ancient and venerable universities, chiefly for the charitable education of intelligent young men for the service of the church.

The necessity for a well-educated ministry of the gospel has never been so generally and powerfully felt any where else as in our own country; and this feeling has been the leading motive in the establishment of by far the larger part of American colleges. "Dreading to leave an illiterate ministry to the churches, when our ministers shall lie in the dust"—such is the language in which the founders of Harvard College describe their own motives in that far-seeing and self-denying enterprise, which they undertook just as soon as they had provided comfortable houses for themselves, and selected convenient places for the worship of God. And sixty years later, Cotton Mather says: "Our fathers saw that without a college to train an able and learned ministry, the church in New England must have been less than a business of an age,—must soon have come to nothing." "Pro Christo et Ecclesia" —*for Christ and the Church*—is to this day the motto of Harvard College, though sadly fallen, alas! from the truth as it is in Jesus.

Yale College, as we have already mentioned, was founded by ministers. It was also founded chiefly for the education of ministers for the colony of Connecticut. It originated, as they tell us, in their sincere regard and zeal for upholding the Protestant religion by a succession of learned and orthodox men.

"Princeton College was founded by the Synod of New York for the purpose of supplying the church with learned and able preachers of the Word." And its paramount religious design and spirit are well expressed in the language of President Witherspoon: "Cursed be all that learning that is contrary to the cross of Christ; cursed be all that learning that is not coincident with the cross of Christ; cursed be all that learning that is not subservient to the cross of Christ."

"Dartmouth College was originated in the warmest spirit, and established in the most elevated principles of Christian piety."

Amherst College grew out of a charity school, which was established for the education of indigent young men for the ministerial and the missionary work. It was born of the prayers, and baptized with the tears, of holy men; and, as in the early history of Harvard, the colonists contributed of their deep poverty, "one bringing a piece of cotton stuff, valued at nine shillings; another, a pewter pot of the same value; a third, a fruit-dish, a spoon, and a large and small salt-cellar;" so, in the founding of Amherst College, the friends of learning and religion in the vicinity brought in the materials, and built up the walls with their own hands, while those at a distance gave in money, or the fruit of their labors, whatever they could spare, which might conduce to the endowment of the institution, and the maintenance of its officers and students. Such self-denials and sacrifices, as were made by the founders of these, and, indeed, most of our colleges, could have proceeded only from religious motives,—only from hearts overflowing with love to Christ and his church. Amherst College was one of the *earliest* institutions that grew up under the influence of the foreign missionary enterprise, and the new impulse which was thus given to all benevolent efforts; and it is, in its character and history a type of a new class of colleges which have sprung up, particularly in the new States, and which may be called emphatically, both as regards their origin and influence, Missionary Colleges.

"Western Reserve College was founded by domestic missionaries, and designed to furnish pastors for the infant churches on the Reserve. Illinois College originated in the union of two independent movements; the one emanating from Home Missionary operations in Illinois, the other from a Society of Inquiry respecting Missions at Yale College. The site of Wabash College was dedicated to God in prayer by its founders kneeling upon the snow in the primeval forest. Marietta College was founded mainly to meet demands for competent teachers and ministers of the gospel."

In fact, nearly all of those institutions which have lived and prospered, and exerted a decided influence, even in our literary and political history, were established by evangelical Christians; and have been taught, for the most part, by evangelical ministers, with a direct and special reference to supplying these churches, and the country and the world, with a learned and pious evangelical ministry. Institutions established by worldly men, for mere worldly objects, have not prospered. Infidelity or irreligion, or no religion, may have founded them, but it could not sustain them; and it has been found necessary to transfer them to the hands of religious guardians and teachers, in order to save them from utter extinction. They have been planned by the wisdom of political sages, and fostered by the wealth and power of the State, but they could not be well managed and governed without the sanctions of religion. They have not won the confidence of parents and guardians, for even irreligious parents do not generally want their children educated in infidelity or impiety; and Christianity, though hated in itself, has been welcomed as a necessary means; though excluded by statutes and constitutions, it has, sooner or later, been admitted to a practical and controlling influence. The history of the University of Virginia, the University of South Carolina, Transylvania University, Dickinson College, Girard College, and, to some extent, Harvard College, had we time to give it, would furnish a satisfactory demonstration of these statements. Baptists and Methodists, Congregationalists and Presbyterians,*—all

* Much the larger number by these last-named denominations. Of the 120 colleges in the United States, 13 are Baptist, 13 Methodist and Episcopalian, and the rest, for the most part, under Congregational and Presbyterian influence.

the evangelical Protestant sects, have their prosperous literary institutions in almost every State of the Union; but infidelity has yet to make its first successful enterprise of this sort; and State policy, State patronage, exclusive of religious influence, cannot show a single flourishing college from the Atlantic and the Great Lakes to the Pacific and the Gulf of Mexico.

These are remarkable facts, especially when considered in connection with the voluntary system, and the entire civil and religious liberty of the American people. A wealthy and powerful establishment,—a church wedded to the State, and enriched by State patronage through successive centuries, we might well suppose, could secure such results. A rich and lordly hierarchy, lording it over the consciences and the estates of the whole people, we should think, might build religious colleges by scores in every part of the country, or might subsidize existing literary institutions, and make them subservient to their views of religion. But that the free voluntary movements of so many different denominations of Christians should have reared a hundred and twenty colleges in different parts of these United States,—many of them in the very infancy of the States, or Provinces, and all within little more than two hundred years after the first settlement of the country; and furnished them with such a succession of learned and pious teachers, and brought them so completely under the controlling influence of a practical Christianity,—this is truly remarkable. It shows that Christianity, with all its divisions and corruptions, still possesses a vital energy, and is still guided and guarded by Him who has all wisdom and all power. It shows that the church is still self-denying in her spirit, and far-reaching in her plans; for nothing but self-denying charity, and far-reaching sagacity, will plant colleges in a new country, when there is a present demand for the necessaries of life, rather than for high mental culture. It shows that there is a natural and mutual affinity between religion and learning; that each alternately seeks the alliance and support of the other, while both are left to the freest action and development. It shows that the American people are imbued with a deep, practical conviction that the college was in its origin, and is in its nature, a religious institution; and must be so, if it would realize its proper literary and political ends. Above all, it proves, as we cannot but believe, and would acknowledge with devout gratitude, that the providence of God has watched over our beloved country in all its history, and guarded it against the dangers to which a youthful and free people are most exposed, as if he intended, in spite of adverse agencies, to preserve this goodly land as a heritage for himself.

The college, then, is the daughter of the church, cherished by her with all a mother's love and care, and self-denial. Has the daughter done any thing in return for the mother? Surely she were an unnatural child if she has made no return of filial love and service to her, to whom she owes all that she has, and all that she is, even to her very existence.

Is it nothing to the church that the system of

popular education, the preparation of text-books, the examination and direction of teachers, and, to so great an extent, the education of the teachers themselves, is in the hands of men who have been trained by Christian scholars in Christian colleges? Is it a small thing for the church, that colleges established by herself, and conducted by her ablest and best men, give tone, in so great a measure, to the literature of the country, and control the reading of the people, not only in books of history and philosophy, and poetry and belles-lettres, but in those magazines and newspapers, which now occupy more and more the pens of our most thoughtful, learned and elegant writers? Is it of little or no consequence to the church that men educated at Christian colleges have, to so great an extent, filled the office of presidents, and governors, and judges, and other civil magistrates in our country, and are also extending their influence every day more widely among the people through the popularization of learning, and those countless applications of science to common life, which are pouring wealth into the bosom of the church for her enterprises of benevolence? Is it nothing to the church, that so many of our lawyers and physicians, and other men of influence in the community, have been taught in college to recognize the divine origin of Christianity, to respect the institutions of religion, and to carry more or less of Christian principles and a Christian spirit with them into the higher walks of life?

These are some of the indirect contributions of colleges to the church. Now let us look at some more direct returns of revenue which she has received from her investments in colleges. Let us see how well they accomplish the more immediate and more prominent object, which the church contemplated in their establishment.

The ministry of this country has been an educated ministry from the first. The earliest ministers in the colonies were of course educated abroad; but soon there rose up schools of the prophets in the wilderness, and the churches looked, nor looked in vain, to Harvard, and Yale, and Nassau Hall, for pastors to feed them with knowledge and understanding. A minister without a thorough college education would scarcely have been tolerated among the Pilgrim Fathers, or their descendants for a hundred years after them. Sects have since sprung up, that for a time eschewed learning, and listened to rant from the pulpit, while they looked in vain for inspiration. But as they have grown older and wiser, even these sects have fallen in with the spirit of the country and the age, and now they, too, demand a learned, as well as pious ministry; now they yield to none in their zeal and liberality for the establishment of colleges and theological seminaries.

The clerical, far beyond either of the other so-called *learned professions*, is actually composed of men of thorough classical education. Half-educated fledglings are fluttering and tumbling into the practice of law and medicine more frequently now, perhaps, than at any former period of our history. But never before was there a smaller relative proportion of uneducated clergymen; never before was the standard of clerical education and attainment so high, and so imperative on all who would enter the sacred office.

It never has been, and is never likely to be, the doctrine of the churches in America, that ministers can be qualified to interpret the sacred oracles without a thorough knowledge of the original languages, or that they can teach the wisdom of God to their fellow-men without being masters of human knowledge.

Nor have the churches looked in vain to the colleges for well-educated ministers. More than half of the graduates of Harvard College, for the first sixty years of its existence, became ministers of the gospel. Nearly three fourths of the graduates of Yale College, for the first twelve years, entered the ministry; and a little less than half during the first thirty years. Almost one half of the alumni of the College of New Jersey became ministers, during the twenty-eight years which preceded the American Revolution. As a country grows older, education becomes more widely diffused, and a smaller proportion of the alumni of the older colleges enter the ministry. But the sacred office has enlisted the talents and learning of from one fifth to one fourth of the entire number of the alumni of these three oldest and most venerable of American colleges, forming an aggregate of nearly four thousand ordained pastors.

Of the eight hundred graduates of Middlebury, and the nine hundred and sixty of Amherst College, nearly one half have devoted themselves to the sacred office. Of the first one hundred and thirteen graduates of Marietta College, sixty-five, or considerably more than half, have become ministers. Of the first sixty-five graduates of Wabash College, forty-five, or more than two thirds, have chosen the same good work. At Illinois College, forty-five out of the first ninety-four alumni, have given themselves to the work of the ministry.

Of the thirty-five thousand graduates from American colleges previous to 1846, as many as eight or nine thousand—nearly one fourth, were preachers of the everlasting gospel. And the other three fourths were educated with them, heard the same lectures and sermons, studied the same text-books of human and divine wisdom, occupied the same rooms, sat in the same seats, walked arm in arm through the same fields and groves,—were, almost of necessity, imbued with *more or less* of the same spirit, and went out to exert a scarcely less important influence upon the interests of the church and the world. So far from being a matter of regret, it affords occasion for devout gratitude, that so many have been educated in so favorable circumstances for the other learned professions, and for stations of influence in society. Who can tell how different their character and influence would have been had they been uneducated, or educated in *anti*-christian or *un*-christian institutions?

Not a few of those new measures and grand movements, which have most seriously affected the church, have had their origin, directly or indirectly, in colleges and universities. The faith and practice of the early Christian church, almost from the time of the apostles and their immediate successors, were greatly modified, —were almost modelled by the schools of philosophy and theology at Alexandria and Antioch, at Edessa and Rome, and Carthage. The strange mixture of truth and error which prevailed in the middle ages was concocted in the schools and libraries of the monasteries, and thence it went forth diffusing life and death throughout Christendom.

The Reformers,—those before the Reformation, as well as the Reformers usually so called,—Wickliffe and Huss, and Reuchlin and Erasmus, Luther and Melancthon, and Bucer and Calvin, and Tyndale and Bilney, and Latimer and Knox, were men trained in the universities, and thus prepared by the providence, as well as the grace of God, for the work which they were destined to accomplish. It was while they were students in the university that new light dawned upon their souls, and the *Greek Testament*, accompanied in several instances by the Latin translation of Erasmus, was, to most of them, the source from which the new light shone. The larger part of them were afterwards professors in the universities, and from these fortresses of learning and influence they hurled their missiles at the corruptions of the papal church; from these centres of illumination, they scattered light over the dark nations. The *Universities of Prague and Wittenberg, of Basle and Lausanne, of Oxford and Cambridge, of Strasburg and St. Andrews, were the birth-places of the Reformation.**

* In proof of this, see D'Aubigne's History of the Reformation, every where, but especially in his fifth volume.

Methodism, which may well be called a second Reformation, which not only gave birth to a new and most efficient Christian organization,—a sort of Protestant society of Jesus,—but infused new life and spirituality into the other denominations of evangelical Christians; Methodism took its rise, received its name, and began its conquests in the University of Oxford. Wesley was for ten years a fellow of Lincoln College, and resisted all the importunities of his friends to leave his fellowship for a curacy, saying, that he could do more for the cause of Christ and the good of men by remaining at Oxford: "the schools of the prophets were there; and was it not a more extensive benefit to sweeten the fountain, than to purify a particular stream?" Among the young men who were intimately associated with Wesley at Oxford were Hervey, the author of those "Meditations" which have aided so many in the cultivation of a heavenly mind; and Whitefield, whose apostolic labors and seraphic eloquence awakened the sleeping Christians of two hemispheres, and led a multitude of lost sinners home to God.

Cambridge was the alma mater of Claudius Buchanan, the author of the "Star in the East," and one of the pioneers in the work of missions to India, and of translating the Scriptures into the vernacular tongues of that great peninsula; also of Henry Martyn, the "Senior Wrangler" * of the University; the disputer with Persian Moollahs, and the translator of

* The highest academical honor.

the New Testament into Persian, whose high scholarship and devoted piety, so harmoniously united, entitle him perhaps to the name of the model missionary. And in and through the same university, "good Dr. Simeon," who gave Martyn the first impulse to a missionary life, long continued to send forth an influence which has leavened a vast number of the ablest preachers and leading members of the Established Church with his own pure faith and active piety.

Nor in enumerating the sources from which a new spiritual life went forth over Great Britain, and thus over Protestant Christendom in the eighteenth century, should we forget to mention the academy or college for the education of dissenting ministers, which was founded by Dr. Watts and Dr. Doddridge, and in which the author of the "Rise and Progress" was also a tutor.

American missions to the heathen had their birth in a little circle of devoted young men, whose prayers have hallowed the rooms, and the very fields about Williams College, and whose example has blessed the nations in every quarter of the globe. The precise locality where Samuel J. Mills and his associates consecrated themselves to a missionary life, we are happy to learn, has been recently identified, and it is to be purchased and set apart as a perpetual memorial of that sacred epoch in the history of the church. A higher monument would mark this place, were monuments any measure of the importance of the events which they commemorate, than rises from any battlefield in the New or the Old World; and Christians, if they had the spirit of Christ and of Christian missions, would go on pilgrimages, not to Bunker's Hill, or Waterloo, but to "the Haystack," near Williams College. The sacred flame, which first began to burn there, has been kept alive on the same and similar altars. American missionaries have not only been graduates of American colleges, but, with few exceptions, they consecrated themselves to the missionary work, while they dwelt in college walls. Facts show that very few decide to become missionaries after leaving college. "From Dartmouth College have gone out twenty-four missionaries to foreign countries; from Amherst, so recently established, thirty-six; from Williams, thirty-three; from Middlebury, twenty-four." * The colleges stand in a no less sacred relation to the cause of Home Missions. In 1850, Amherst had as many as fifty home missionaries in the field.

The men for all our benevolent enterprises must come from the colleges, and will carry through life very much of the character and spirit they had when in college. Students give more *money* for benevolent objects, in proportion to their means, than almost any other community. This may not be so with all colleges and higher seminaries, but we know it is so in more than one. We have seen the poor student throw his last quarter into the contribution box, saying (with a sublime faith, not perhaps to be imitated by all, but worthy of universal admiration), "There is all the money I have in the world. I will have that safe."

But money is the smallest contribution which is

* Dr. Park's Address before the Western College Society. The number of missionaries from Amherst is now (1854) about 50.

made by students in college to the cause of Christian charity. They have first given themselves to the Lord and to his work, wherever and whatever it may be. With a faith, like that of Abraham, they have been willing to leave their country, not knowing whither they go, while with a love, like that of Christ they have offered up themselves on the altar of reconciliation between God and their fellow-men.

The commencement of the new era of benevolence, —the era of Missionary and Bible, and Tract and Education Societies—was marked by the establishment of an unusual number, we might almost say, a new kind of colleges; and they in turn have sustained and furthered the various forms of associated benevolence, with unwonted zeal and devotion. At the same time (to their honor be it said, as well as in truth and justice), some of the older institutions have caught not a little of the new spirit, and lavished the accumulated treasures of their wisdom and their influence in the support of those moral and religious enterprises which are the glory of the age.

Those revivals of religion, which so illustrate and bless our times, have prevailed in colleges with greater frequency and power than in any other communities; and who can calculate the good influences, direct and indirect, which revivals in colleges have exerted on the churches? How many ministers and magistrates, professional men and men of influence, have *there been born* into the kingdom of Christ; and how many more *re*-converted, so that, like Peter, they could strengthen their brethren? How many, while members of college, have caught the spirit of revivals and of missions, and carried it home to the church to which they belong, and with the characteristic ardor and *strength of young men* in a course of education, diffused it through the place of their nativity? And when such men have been settled in the ministry, their own churches have been revival churches, and missionary churches; the life of the communities around them, and the light of this dark world. It has been estimated that one revival of religion, which took place in Yale College, under the presidency of Dr. Dwight, raised up ministers who were instrumental of the conversion of fifty thousand souls in one generation.

Thus, it appears that marked eras in the history of the church have usually been marked eras in the history of colleges, from the establishment of the first seminary in the early Christian church to the foundation of the last college in our western wilderness. The progress of the churches has been *registered*, so to speak, and their attainments have been secured and perpetuated by the colleges, while, in turn, every new wave of thought, and tide of feeling in the colleges, has had its corresponding wave and tide in the churches. The stream will not permanently rise higher than the fountain. The fountain determines the quality, as well as the height of the stream. The college and the church are alternately or mutually fountain and stream. More frequently the impulse originates in the college. It was so in the Reformation. It was so with the Oxford heresy. The Unitarian defection in New England originated perhaps with the churches, or rather with their pastors, but it has been perpetuated by Harvard College. The tide rose in the churches till it burst open the gates and inundated the college, but now it has turned, and is flowing back, more gradually, but not less powerfully, and even more effectively, from the college into the churches and the community. Let all our colleges become like Harvard, and Unitarianism would overflow the country. Or let them become such schools of infidelity as Jefferson and Girard would fain have established ; and, unless they are abandoned and their gates closed, the next generation will forsake the religion of their fathers, and the churches will be deserted by the people. Or let our ministers and men of influence be uneducated, or half educated, and errors and heresies will spring up like thorns and briers in a neglected field ; for it is men who are untaught in history (especially the history of doctrines), and undisciplined in their mental and moral faculties, whose minds have been the hot-beds of theological error in every age of the church. To pray for the colleges, then, is to pray for the churches, for an educated and devoted ministry,—for a pure and Protestant Christianity,—for foreign and home missions,—for evangelical revivals of religion ; in a word, for churches, that shall live and work, and propagate a sound faith, lively hope and impartial charity through the world.

CHAPTER IX.

College Life—Its Temptations and Dangers—Its Moral and Religious Advantages—The College a unique Community—Its essential Characteristics—A Community of Young Men—Four years together, from Seventeen to Twenty-one—Constant Contact with their Teachers—Subjects of Investigation—Recitation—Morning and Evening Prayers—Public Worship and Preaching on the Sabbath—Influence on each other—College Friendships—Enticements of Sinners—Counsels and Prayers of Pious Friends and of the Church—Fewer Dangers and more Safeguards than in most other Communities—Habits of Industry—System—Employment of Time—Christian Teachers—Pious Students—Facilities for Religious Improvement—Decisive Period—Same Facilities fruitful either of Good or Evil—Possibility and Importance of turning them all to Good—Prayer for immediate Conversion of Students.

THE college is a unique community. It has sentiments and usages, not to say a law and a dialect, peculiar to itself. These peculiarities are partly traditional, and therefore somewhat arbitrary, and partly the natural result of the elements of which it is composed, and the manner in which it is organized.

The essential characteristics of college, as they result naturally from its elements and organization, are, that it is a community of young men at that age when their character is most susceptible of being formed and established, living by themselves, though under the constant oversight and influence of their teachers, and engaged during an entire period of four years in such studies as are adapted to discipline their minds and form their habits for future usefulness. Four years, from seventeen to twenty-one (for that is perhaps about the average age), spent in such pursuits, and under such circumstances, must contribute largely to the formation of their whole character, intellectual, social, moral and religious. Quick to perceive, bold to think and reason, yet easy to be persuaded and influenced, their minds and hearts are open to teachers whom they respect ; and those teachers are in direct public communication with them some three or four hours of every day, besides frequent private interviews of a more personal and confidential nature. Their instructors commune with them on the most delightful and ennobling subjects. They introduce them to the familiar acquaintance of the historians and poets, and orators and philosophers of antiquity ; the heroes and martyrs of ancient history, the wisest and best men of every country and every age. They lead them back to the secret springs of nature, and explore with them the arcana of mathematical and physical science. They conduct them to the deeper springs and remoter arcana of their own spiritual being, and teach them, in the knowledge of themselves, to lay the foundations of all knowledge. They teach them to look through nature and man to the God of man and nature ; and not only do they teach this in the recitation-room, but every morning and every evening, as well as twice every Sabbath, they lead them to the lively oracles of the only living and true God, and go with them directly into the presence of Him, in whom are hid all the treasures of wisdom and knowledge. And never was there an audience more attentive to an able and eloquent preacher, or more susceptible of impression from solemn and weighty truth ; never a congregation more easily and entirely swayed by the truth and the Spirit of God, like the waving corn by every wind of heaven, than is a congregation of college students in a season of unusual religious interest.

The minds and hearts of students are peculiarly turned to each other, as wax to the seal. And they are in perpetual contact, acting and reacting each upon the other, from week to week, and month to month, term after term, and year after year. There is no community like college for the propagation of influence ; like so many particles of a fluid, if one is at rest, all are at rest—if one moves, all are on the move : impulses are communicated without delay or resistance, and motion is simultaneous through the whole body. At the same time, there is no community where impressions are deeper, influences more permanent, attachments more enduring. There are no friendships like college friendships. Many a David and a Jonathan have there had their hearts knit together, like the heart of one man, in mutual, equal, disinterested love, which death could not sever. The name of classmate and room-mate grows more and more sacred, as other attachments fade away, and we draw near to the end of all earthly connections. Those who have been members of the same division, or the same literary society, however widely separated, and however different their lot, will never forget each other,—will watch and follow each other through all the vicissitudes of life to the very borders of the grave. Hence it is that those reunions, which bring together college acquaintance and friends at commencement, are so delightful; and to none more delightful than to those who have outlived other connections and attachments, and stand trembling, almost alone, on the borders of eternity. Hence, also, the peculiar *importance* of his friendships to the character and happiness of the young man in college, and the special necessity of being on his guard in the choice of his companions. His ardent and susceptible nature is easily, quickly attached; and yet an attachment which thus springs up in a day, if strengthened by four years' association, will grow into a part of himself, and become a permanent element in his character and his very being.

In such a community, where influence is so easily propagated, and yet so lasting in its effects, temptation must, of course, have peculiar power. The ardent and inexperienced youth, when he first enters college, is exposed to a fiery trial. He will be sure to meet with the enticements of sinners, for in the best colleges, as in the best towns, there are bad young men, and sin and misery always *love company*, because they always *need* it, that they may escape, if possible, from their wicked and wretched selves. He will be tempted to idleness, and idleness every where is the parent of vice. He will be tempted to eating and carousing, and card-playing, and blasphemy of sacred things, not all at once, but as fast as he can bear the shock; and in some colleges, he will be enticed to the perpetration of vices that are yet more fatal than any of these, to the body and the soul. He needs, therefore, to come armed with the counsels and prayers of his friends, and the church of God. He needs to be followed up by those counsels and prayers, by the watch and care of pious students, and by the frequent warnings and earnest supplications of faithful teachers. He needs most of all, and best of all, the safeguard of religious principle and experience ; to begin with it, if possible, but if he comes to college without it, to seek it for himself, and have it sought for him by others, with all, and more than all, the assiduity with which they guard his intellectual training ; with all, and more than all, the zeal and perseverance with which evil companions and wicked spirits will entice him to sin. And after all that is done for him, he will go astray, and be lost for time and eternity, unless the grace of God restrain his wayward will, and win and conquer his depraved heart. Those who have stood long on these watch-towers know well the dangers of the coast, and cannot but raise a warning voice,—cannot but point to breakers along a shore, which they have seen thickly strewn with wrecks of the proudest ships and the most precious cargoes.

Do any of our readers say, if this is so, it is not good to send a young man to college ? But where are not the young in danger ? Where else can anxious parents send their sons, and feel that they are exposed to fewer temptations ? Where else, indeed, will they find so small a proportion of profane and licentious youth, and those under so many daily, and almost hourly restraints upon their evil propensities ? Where else so many young men, who are truly pious, and who will exert on those sons a truly Christian influence? What other community is there where revivals are so frequent, conversions so numerous, professors of religion so much in the ascendency, moral and religious influences so constantly brought to bear on every individual? In one word, where is the city or town, or neighborhood—we might almost ask, where is the *family*, in which there are so many helps to virtue and piety, as in our best colleges?

College life tends directly to *habits of industry, regularity* and *system;* and these constitute the strongest barriers against dissipation; these cast up a broad and open highway to every virtue. Every day has its proper occupations, almost every hour brings its assigned duties. Thrice every day the bell summons the student to meet his instructor in public recitation; twice to appear before God in the sanctuary for public worship. The morning prayer-bell forbids late rising; the morning recitation almost forbids late carousing and deep drinking the night before; and at no hour of the day, can he wander very far from his duty without being called back by that faithful monitor. The studies are not only occupying and engrossing, but interesting and instructive. While they discipline the mind, they also enlighten the conscience, and purify the heart, and inculcate by precept and example sacred lessons of wisdom and duty. The instructors are men of high moral and Christian excellence, who cannot forget often to remind them, that the fear of the Lord is the beginning of wisdom, and to depart from evil is understanding; and that though they have *all knowledge*, and could speak with the *tongues* of men and angels, and are destitute of holy love, they are nothing. Very many of the students, also—in not a few colleges, the majority—are young men of Christian principle and Christian spirit, who aspire to the office of ambassadors of Christ, and who, even in college, are nobly ambitious to turn many to righteousness. Such opportunities for Christian communion and social prayer, and mutual encouragement in the divine life ; so many facilities for the cultivation of virtue and piety in those who have the good seed already implanted in their hearts, and so many helps and inducements to commence a religious life in those who have not,—are scarcely to be found any where else.

These causes conspire to render college, notwithstanding its temptations and dangers, a comparatively safe place for young men. We are persuaded that parents, who are obliged to send their sons from home, can hardly send them to a safer place. It is far safer than the city or large village. Boys are ruined by being sent to college, but they are ruined in far greater number and proportion by being sent away to business. One in four (we state it on the authority of a mayor of one of our great cities), one in four of the young men who go from the country into the city to engage in business, make shipwreck, not merely of business prospects, but of character and happiness. Not one in ten of those who enter college so degrade and destroy themselves ; and a large part of these were effectually corrupted before they left home.

The same causes, however, conspire also to render the college course a great crisis in a young man's life.

If, in spite of such powerful influences for good, he *does* leave college a votary of Bacchus or Venus, he is in great danger of remaining such through life. If he is not converted in college, or, at least, so deeply impressed with religious convictions and purposes as ere long to take a decided stand as a Christian,* there is a fearful probability that he will live and die an unconverted man. If he ever decides to become a minister, in all probability it will be in college. If he devotes himself to the missionary work, he will probably do it in college. Few who fail to make that decision as early as the college course, ever stand on missionary ground. His standard of piety in college will be likely to be his standard of piety through life. Not but that he who is a devoted Christian in college will grow in knowledge and in grace in the seminary and in the ministry; but if he is *not* a devoted Christian in college, he will not be in the seminary, in the ministry, or any where else. Such is the uniform testimony which comes back to college in letters from the theological seminary and from the parsonage. Such is the observation and experience of those who have paid particular attention to the subject; and such we might expect to be the general fact from the nature of the case: for those who can withstand such a concentration of good influences as are brought to bear for so many years on the students in the colleges of New England at so early,

* Those who have sown the good seed in students' hearts, "weeping" all the way through their college course, are sometimes (experience would justify us in saying not unfrequently) rejoiced at hearing, that it has sprung up *soon* after they left college.

so susceptible and so critical a period of their lives, must incur a fearful amount of guilt, and contract a dreadful power of resistance. How earnest and importunate, then, should be the prayers of all the friends of learning and religion for the conversion of young men in college! How should pious parents especially wrestle with the Angel of the Covenant for the immediate conversion of their sons, saying, I *cannot,—will* not let thee go, except thou bestow this great blessing.

The very circumstances that prove temptations or hindrances to some, may, and do become helps and encouragements to others. Wherever there are peculiar facilities for evil, there also there are, or may be, peculiar facilities for good. Good and evil both dwell in the same hearts, appeal to the same natural susceptibilities, spread according to the same general laws, are propagated by the same agencies and instrumentalities. The same agency that is mighty to do evil, may be made mighty to do good. The channel in which evil flows most easily, may be made to flow full and strong with good. This is a universal law, and nowhere is it more strikingly verified than in college. In some institutions, sometimes, every engine of power seems to be employed for evil purposes. Every channel seems to be filled with evil influences. In others, good and evil are strangely mixed, and almost evenly balanced. In some colleges, at some times, at least, good seems to be entirely in the ascendency. Literature, science, society, conversation,—intellectual, social and moral influence,—all tend towards virtue and piety, heaven and God. The perpetuation of this, or something like this, is all that is necessary to make colleges a heaven on earth; a heaven of knowledge, a heaven of love, a heaven of holiness and a heaven of happiness. Such an appropriation of all the peculiarities of college life, of all the enginery of college power, of all the channels of college influence to Christ and his church,—such a sanctification of all the young men with all the powers and susceptibilities of their nature, and all the facilities afforded by their circumstances and relations, that they may be holiness to the Lord,—such is the consummation towards which officers and pious students, and friends of education and friends of religion, should all look. It is for this that they should labor in the use of all possible and suitable means. It is for this that we invite their earnest, believing and persevering prayers.

CHAPTER X.

Revivals and Conversions in College—More frequent than in other Communities—Statistics of Yale, Dartmouth, Middlebury, Amherst, Illinois, Marietta, Wittemburg—Edwards, Hopkins, and other distinguished men converted in College—Number of Conversions in College equal to half the number of Alumni, who have become Ministers—One fourth of the Individuals who enter the Ministry converted in College—Number of Professors of Religion and Candidates for the Ministry now in several Colleges—Proportion to the whole number of Students—Need of more frequent and powerful Revivals—Revivals in harmony with the Nature of Man, with the Spirit of the Age, with the Constitution, and Circumstances of Young Men in College—Scenes witnessed during Revivals in College—Henry Lyman—Bela B. Edwards—A Revival every year for every Class, as it enters—Every thing else in College periodical, why not Revivals?—Favorable to Study—Every thing attended to in its Season, and by Rule, why not Revivals?—Why only one third, or less, Professors of Religion, and one sixth Ministers?—Mount Holyoke Seminary.

THERE are very few churches in which revivals and conversions have been so frequent and so numerous; there are very few communities in which so large a proportion of the population, especially of the young men, are professors of religion, as in the colleges of New England and the Northern States. This has already been asserted or implied in former chapters. So important a fact, if it be a fact, is worthy of more particular consideration; and, if it be doubted, it admits of a ready and ample substantiation. In the space of ninety-six years, beginning with the great revival of 1741, and ending in 1837, there were twenty revivals in Yale College, in fourteen of which five hundred students were hopefully converted ; and during the last twenty-five years of this same period, there were thirteen special revivals, or one every two years, besides several other seasons of more than usual religious interest. Indeed, for *thirty* years previous to 1848, revivals occurred in Yale College, on an average, about once in two years ; and in one of these revivals, there were a hundred hopeful conversions. What church has enjoyed as many revivals in the same time ? Among the subjects of the revivals in Yale College were Evarts, Cornelius, Nevins, Hopkins, Edwards, and perhaps Dwight and Bellamy ; and a multitude of Christian soldiers, only inferior to those greater leaders of the sacramental host. Who can calculate the influence of so many revivals in which such men were, from time to time, brought into the kingdom of God and the ministry of reconciliation !

In Dartmouth College, in the space of sixty-five years, nine extensive revivals of religion were enjoyed ; the converts in six of these numbered one hundred and seventy ; and among them were distinguished ministers, leading missionaries, presidents and professors in colleges and theological seminaries, and other men of high standing and influence in the church and the State. Middlebury College has been blessed in forty years with ten revivals,—some of them of great power. During the first twenty-five years of its history, every class but one was permitted to share in a religious awakening, and some classes received three or four such visits of mercy while in college.

No class has ever yet left Amherst College without

witnessing a powerful revival of religion, and scarce a year has passed without some special interest in the church, and more or less conversions. During the thirty years of its existence, there have been from two hundred and fifty to three hundred hopeful conversions. Of these converts, more than one hundred have been ministers, fifteen have been missionaries, twenty-eight officers of colleges and theological seminaries; and several were young men of genius and great promise, who died before entering upon a profession. Their names, were we allowed to specify some of them, would illustrate, even more than their number, the unspeakable value of a revival in college. We can only mention among those who, we trust, are now in heaven, such names as those of Prof. Bela B. Edwards, Prof. William A. Peabody, Story Hebard of the Syrian Mission, Timothy Dwight, who had devoted himself to the cause of missions, but died before leaving the country; Rev. George P. Smith of Worcester, Rev. Amos Bullard of Barre, Rev. William Bradford Homer, —names precious in the records of young American ministers. All but one of these were *tutors* in Amherst College.

In the first twelve years of the history of Amherst College, there were four revivals; in Illinois College, six in the first eighteen years; in Marietta College, seven in fifteen years; in Wabash College, nine in fourteen years; and no class has passed through its collegiate course there without having witnessed from one to four revivals. Similar to these has been the history of all those missionary colleges which are under the patronage of the Western College Society.

"Facts seem to authorize the opinion," says the Fifth Report of the Society, "that the number of conversions which have occurred in the whole history of Yale College would nearly equal one half of the whole number of its graduates who have entered the ministry." In Amherst College, the number of conversions is known to bear a still larger proportion to the number of ministers, the whole number of conversions having been at least two hundred and fifty, and the whole number of ministers four hundred and thirty-five. For a period of twenty-two years in Middlebury College, one half of the pious graduates are believed to have been converted while in connection with college. "From some investigations that have been made, it would seem that the number of hopeful conversions among the youth of the colleges aided by the Western College Society is full one half of the whole number who have devoted themselves to the ministry. It would not follow from this, however, that one half of the latter number was actually composed of those particular individuals."

This suggests another question, which deserves, and has received the attentive consideration of officers in college, and others, who are interested in this subject,—namely, what proportion of the individuals who have actually entered the ministry, were hopefully converted in college? The writer has recently examined the triennial catalogue of Amherst College, marking the names of all that are known to have commenced their Christian life in college. Of the four hundred and thirty-five who have entered the ministry, one hundred have thus been identified as having been hopefully converted in college; and it cannot be doubted that were it possible, after the lapse of thirty years, to identify the entire number, they would be found to compose one fourth of all who have entered the ministry. It does not appear that investigations have been made covering the whole history of other colleges, and relating to this particular question. But during *limited* periods, about the same ratio has been found to hold in several other colleges. About one fourth of all the alumni of Williams College, who entered the ministry during a period of twenty-five years, were converted in college. The same is true of all the alumni of Dartmouth College, who entered the ministry from twenty-nine classes, commencing with 1809. During the presidency of Dr. Bates at Middlebury, about one fifth of the alumni who became ministers were considered as fruits of revivals in colleges; and it is believed that the proportion was still greater, before the Education Society sent large numbers into every class.

Another question of great interest, is the number of *professors of religion*, and of *candidates for the ministry*. The present state* of eleven colleges in New England is exhibited in the following table,† which is the result of recent correspondence between the So-

* February, 1853.

† Prepared by the Sec. of the Am. Educ. Soc.

ciety of Inquiry in Amherst College and similar societies in other institutions.

	Students.	Professors of Religion.	Preparing for the Ministry.
Bowdoin College, . . .	152	37	
Waterville College, . .	86	46	18
University of Vermont, .	123	30	25
Middlebury College, .	60	35	17
Amherst College, ...	187	113	77
Williams College, . .	207	106	71
Brown University, . . .	243	80	35
Harvard College, . .	319	30	
Yale College, ...	446	130	70
Wesleyan University, .	103	78	35
Dartmouth College, . .	237	60	
	2163	745	348

If the blanks, which occur under the head "Preparing for the Ministry," were filled, it would doubtless add some fifty to the number. By this table, it appears that about one third of the young men connected with our colleges are professors of religion, and a little more than one half of these, or one sixth of the whole, are preparing for the ministry.

The ratio of professors of religion to the whole number of students in Amherst College, has always been more than half,—now it is three fifths; sometimes it has been two thirds. Often nearly all the members of the upper classes are professors of religion; at the present time,* all but two of the Senior Class are hopefully pious. And by far the larger part of the professors of religion have always been studying with a view to preach the gospel.

* 1853.

In Western Reserve College, the ratio of pious students at different times has varied from two thirds to four fifths. In Wabash College, of five hundred and seventy-one students that had been connected with all the departments previous to 1848, two hundred and twenty were either pious when they entered, or became so after joining the college ; and of the fifty-two who had been graduated, thirty-nine were hopefully pious. Of the one hundred graduates of Marietta College, previous to 1848, sixty were hopefully pious when they entered, twenty-three were hopefully converted in college, and only seventeen graduated without hope in Christ. In 1848, there were in Knox College (the college proper) fifty-two attending members ; of these, thirty-eight were professors of religion ; and of the two classes that had then graduated, all but one were professors of religion, and were either preparing for the ministry, or engaged in teaching.

Now what other communities are there in which revivals of religion occur so frequently, where so large a proportion are hopefully pious, and where so large a proportion of those who remain only four years, *become* hopefully pious during their stay ? Certainly not at the West, under the eaves of our Western colleges. No, not even in the East, in the vicinity of the colleges of New England. Let the comparison be carefully made between the colleges of New England and the best religious societies in New England, and the result will speak volumes for the religious character and influence of the colleges. Let the comparison be made between the young *men* in other communities and the young men in college, and the contrast will be still more striking. This is no ground of boasting. But it does show the comparative safety of our colleges, and the wisdom of sending our sons to them, if we would see them converted. It is occasion for devout thanksgiving to God, that while his wise providence has intrusted these institutions to such hands, his grace has infused such a sanctifying power into these fountains of influence. And it calls for earnest prayer to the Author of all good, that these sacred influences may be perpetuated and increased, till these fountains shall send forth none but pure streams.

And as an essential means to this end, revivals of religion of still greater frequency and power should be an especial object of prayer and effort. Revivals are in accordance with the analogy of nature, which has its seasons of revivification and rapid growth followed by seasons of ripening fruit and maturing strength. They are in harmony with the nature of man, who requires alternate seasons of activity and repose ; of stirring labor and excitement on the one hand, and on the other, of tranquil enjoyment and sober reflection ; each in turn preparing the body and the mind for the other, and both in their due season imparting health and vigor to the system, and conspiring to produce the largest possible results. Revivals accord especially with the habits and spirit of the present age, which is an age of excitement, of division of labor, of associated feeling and action, of concentrated effort, and hurried enterprise and rapid locomotion ; and religion, if it is to keep pace at all with business or pleasure, or sin, must fall in more or less with the movements of men and things. Revivals of religion are peculiarly adapted to the constitution and the circumstances of young men in college,—with their quick impulses and lively sympathies, their love of excitement and activity,—the exciting and engrossing nature of their pursuits also, and the peculiar force of their temptations. Occupation and excitement are to them a necessity. If they are not, at particular times, specially excited by the thoughts of religion, they will be always engrossed, if not by something hurtful, at least by something not so useful, not so important, not so essential to their temporal and eternal well-being. They are remarkably susceptible on this great subject. Serious thoughts, anxious inquiry and earnest prayer spread through a community of college students with the rapidity and the power of an electric shock. Every eye is open, every ear attentive, every conscience awake, every heart alive to this one-engrossing interest. Dissipation ceases, amusement is forgotten, the ball-ground and gymnasium even are forsaken, silence reigns through the rooms and halls, broken only by the voice of prayer. Now and then perhaps a number band together for rioting and uproar, possibly to make sport of sacred things. But it is like the revelling of Belshazzar and his court over the sacred vessels of the house of the Lord ; they see a handwriting on the wall, and their knees smite together : the next day, they are found penitent and believing before the cross, and in a few years they are preaching the gospel in the far West, or publishing the glad tidings of salvation to the more remote nations of the East; or perhaps dying a martyr's death among the savages in some tropical isle.* Another company preferring a more respectable way of ridiculing serious things, invite a tutor † to hold a meeting with them. He complies with their invitation, and those who came to mock, remain to pray. Scenes like these send a new thrill of wonder and joy through the whole community. The kingdom of heaven suffereth violence, and the violent take it by force. All seem to be pressing into it; and in the course of two or three weeks, the conversions are counted by scores. Then the intense excitement gradually subsides. But the impressions are permanent; the fruit remains. Under proper instruction, and watch and care, the converts in college are found to hold out as well as any other congregation. Oh, if we could but take our Christian readers with us from room to room, and hall to hall, when such events are occurring, and let them witness with their own eyes these thrilling scenes, and sympathize in their own hearts with these marvellous transformations; or could we place them on some high vantage-ground, where they could not only take in at a glance the whole literary community, whether retired within their closets, or gathered in little circles for prayer and religious conference, or assembled in the house of God on the Sabbath, but where they could also catch a glimpse of the future history of those converted youths, and trace the results of one such season of religious interest, then they could not withhold their prayers for revivals in colleges.

* Henry Lyman. † Bela B. Edwards.

Revivals of religion are not yet so frequent, or so pure or powerful, even in college, as it is greatly to be desired they should be. Why should not a revival occur every year, that every class, as it enters, may also enter the school of Christ; and as it advances from year to year in the college course, may receive a fresh anointing of the Holy Spirit, and so all their studies be pursued in his illuminating presence, and holiness to the Lord be written on every hall, on the door of every room, and at the entrance to every heart? Then would they indeed *know all things* which it chiefly concerns them to know, having received an unction from the Holy One.

Every thing else in college is periodical. This is one of the most striking characteristics of college life. Why, then, should not special attention to the subject of personal religion be periodical? Classes enter and leave every year. Why should they not be converted every year? Why should this not be distinctly contemplated, expressly aimed at, and specially provided for, like all the other regular exercises and arrangements of the institution? This would not be inconsistent with the design of such institutions, or conflict with the studies or literary attainments of the student. On the contrary, it would harmonize with that design; nay, more, it is due to that design: for colleges in their original plan and intention were meant to be religious institutions. And it would greatly further the advancement of students in learning; for the principles and spirit of true religion are the surest guide, the strongest stimulus to the right use of time, to the best improvement of talents and opportunities, and to the most successful prosecution of all useful knowledge; insomuch, that not only theologians and reformers, but philosophers and scholars have indorsed the maxim: "Bene orasse est bene studuisse;"—to have prayed well, is to have studied well.

Such a systematic attention to the subject of personal religion would fall in not only with the design, but with the general arrangements of a college. Every thing else there is done by rule and system; every thing else has its allotted time and place. Why should not the earliest suitable time, and the first proper place—why should not the best time and the best place in every year be given to the greatest and best object, which, when assigned its proper time and place, furthers every other right aim, and secures every true interest? The whole economy of Nature and Providence is regulated by times and seasons. Why should it not be so with religion? There is a time to sow, and a time to reap; and these in Nature are annual. Why should it not be so in the church and the college? Why should any church entertain a prejudice against systematic and periodical efforts to secure the revival of religion and the salvation of souls, while they have a time and a place, a period and a system, for every thing else that they do, and do to any purpose? Above all, why should this prejudice be harbored in college, which involves—which may almost be said to consist in—a series of periodical action and repose, and in which, from its earliest establishment, it has always been intended that religion should hold the first place? Why, we ask again, should not every year witness a revival in college, and every class, as it enters on a new stadium, receive a fresh anointing from on high? Why should any class graduate, we do not say without a revival, but without having witnessed as many revivals as they have spent years in college? Why should any individual leave these schools of the church unconverted? Why should only one third of the members of college in New England —only one third upon an average, and far less in many colleges—be professors of religion; and why should only one half of these professors of religion—only one sixth of the whole number of the students—devote themselves to the ministry of the everlasting gospel?

Is this the highest consummation that can be conceived as possible? this the largest result that can be made real, in institutions founded by the church for the express purpose of raising up ministers of the gospel? Is it not—after all that we have said in the way of congratulation and thanksgiving—is it not a sad falling below the proper standard of such institutions, a melancholy failure to accomplish their highest and best end? Must it be so of necessity, and for ever? When other professions are full to overflowing, and men cannot be found to supply our own churches in New England, still less to preach the gospel to the destitute in the new settlements and among the far-off heathen; when the world is one vast open field that invites the sickle, and the harvest (and *such* a harvest! a harvest of immortal souls, which angels would gladly gather) is perishing for want of laborers,—must five sixths of the alumni of New England colleges devote their energies to secular pursuits? It is incredible on the face of it. From the nature of the case, we know there is, there *must* be more power in the instructions and example of college officers, in the prayers and efforts of the Christian church, in the gospel and grace of God, than has yet been brought to bear on the conversion of young men in college. And facts show that larger results have been realized when greater and more direct efforts have been made for this express purpose. At Mount Holyoke, and some other female seminaries, where this is made a direct object of prayer and effort early in the year, revivals occur every year, and nearly all the new pupils are hopefully converted. In some of the missionary colleges of the West, revivals have occurred almost every year. In a still larger number, more or less conversions occur every year near the beginning of the course.

When young men first leave home and parents and friends, and enter strangers on college life, they are naturally thoughtful and serious; they feel the need of divine teaching and assistance, and almost spontaneously cry unto God, "Our Father, be thou the guide of our youth." Under these circumstances, if they were taken under the especial watch and care of the officers and pious students, and kindly warned and entreated, and led by the hand of Christian friendship, and compassed about with an atmosphere of prayer; and if, at the same time, they were borne on the arms of faith and prayer by the whole church,—who can doubt that a revival would occur every year, and almost the whole class be converted at the commencement of the college course. How different then would be the spirit and the result of all their studies, and how different a place would college then be ; how much more a realization of the beau ideal of a Christian college, than even the most favored of all these favored institutions now is.

The possibility of realizing such a result by more prayer and effort will receive further confirmation, as we proceed, in our next chapter, to speak of the improvement that has already taken place in the spiritual condition of our colleges, since they have been made a subject of special prayer by the churches.

CHAPTER XI.

Concert of Prayer for Colleges—More frequent Revivals of Religion attendant on increased Prayer in the Churches—Increase of *Italics* in the Triennials—State of Religion in Yale College the last half of the last Century—In 1783—In 1795—At the close of the Century—Compared with 1820, 1831, &c.—Dartmouth College—The year 1820 a new Era in History of Colleges—New Colleges—Concert of Prayer—Its Origin and Results—Answers to Prayer—Revivals for the most part soon after the Concert—More Prayer likely to be followed with still more glorious Results—Special Necessity for Prayer at the present Time—Diminished Supply of Ministers for a few years past—Causes—Increased Demand—Extreme Exigency—Fearful Responsibility—Prayer to the Lord of the Harvest.

THE religious history of American colleges during the present century, especially when contrasted with the latter part of the previous century, is full of instruction, and full of encouragements to prayer on the part of all the friends of learning and religion. We get some idea of the change that has been going on during this period, by simply looking over the triennial catalogues of the colleges, and noticing the gradual increase of *italics*, which mark the names of ministers, from the latter part of the eighteenth century down to the middle of the nineteenth. Compare, for instance, the last decade of the eighteenth century on the Yale triennial with the ten years from 1830 to 1840, or from 1840 to 1850, on the same triennial. A comparison of all the triennials that extend over the last quarter of the last century with the triennials of the colleges that have originated in the quarter of a century just past, would furnish a still more striking contrast.

But when we inquire more particularly into the relative frequency of revivals, and the proportion of professors of religion, we are surprised and delighted with the improvement. Take, for instance, some facts in the religious history of Yale College. Through all the last half of the last century, only three revivals are recorded. It was a period of declension in the *churches* also, and of infidelity and immorality in the country, when the disastrous effects of our own Revolutionary War (we mean, of course, the *moral* and *religious* effects), and still more of the French Revolution, infected, like a plague, all classes of the people. In the first twenty years of the nineteenth century, there were four revivals; in the next sixteen years, there were nine; and from 1820 to 1848, there was, upon an average, about one in every two years.

In 1795, only eleven under-graduates are known to have been professors of religion; about four years after, the number was reduced to four or five; and at one communion, only a single under-graduate was present, the others being out of town. A surviving member of the class of 1783,* remembers only three professors of religion in the class of 1782, and only three or four each in several of the preceding classes. In his own class, which was blessed with a revival, there were eleven. In the darkest time, just at the close of the century, there was only about one profes-

* The venerable Rev. Payson Williston, of Easthampton, Mass.

sor of religion to a class! The state of things was no better, however, in the *churches*. A young man who belonged to the church in that day was almost a miracle. Even after the remarkable revival in 1802, when, out of two hundred and sixty students, about one third were hopefully converted, the number of professed Christians in all the classes was again reduced to fifteen.

But with 1820 begins a new era in Yale College. From that time, there was a revival of more or less power every year for five years; and the college church has never again sunk so low in numbers or strength. The year 1831 was a memorable year in the history of revivals, both in colleges and churches. There were revivals in nineteen colleges; the greatest number (and some of them the most powerful) that have ever been known. As a natural consequence of revivals in the churches, an unusual proportion of those who entered college in 1832 were hopefully pious; fifty out of ninety in the Freshman Class of Yale College; and one of the professors, in a letter written at the time, speaks of it as a striking fact, and a new era in the history of literary institutions.

Similar facts might be stated in regard to other colleges. About one fourth of the graduates of Dartmouth College became ministers from 1790 to 1800, and only one fifth from 1800 to 1810; but between 1810 and 1830, the proportion increased to one third.

The year 1820, which we have already spoken of as marking a transition in the religious history of Yale College, introduces a new era in the history of colleges generally, and particularly of revivals in colleges. It was about this time, that an increased interest in the education of ministers and missionaries led to the establishment of colleges in more rapid succession, and with more express reference to this object; Waterville College and Western University in 1820, Amherst College and Columbia (D. C.) in 1821, Miami University in 1824, Western Reserve in 1828, Illinois College in 1830, Wabash in 1832, Marietta in 1833, &c.

It was also about this time that the Concert of Prayer for Colleges began to be observed. The origin and some of the results of this important movement are given as follows, by the Secretary of the Western College Society.

"*Origin of the Concert.*—This was a spirit of supplication among Christians in behalf of colleges and theological seminaries, created by statistical information in respect to them, published from time to time in the Annual Reports of the American Education Society. A concert of prayer was first established to be observed every Sabbath morning. Frequent and powerful revivals of religion in colleges followed, which seemed very much like answers to the supplications offered at these seasons of prayer. The children of God were encouraged to persevere, and finally, in consequence of a circular issued, with the knowledge and approbation of the directors of the American Education Society, the last Thursday of February, 1823, was set apart by many of the friends of Zion as 'a season of fasting and special prayer, that God will pour out his Spirit on the colleges of our country the present year more powerfully than ever before.'

"*Answers to Prayer.*—Subsequent to the establishment of the Sabbath Morning Concert, the Spirit of God was poured out, and cheering results witnessed. From 1820 to 1823 inclusive, there were revivals in fourteen different institutions; in 1824 and 1825, in five different colleges; in 1826, in six; in 1827, in four; in 1828, in five; and in 1831, in nineteen colleges, resulting in the hopeful conversion of between three hundred and fifty and four hundred students. In one of the colleges, the revival commenced on the very day of the concert. In 1832, some few institutions were blessed with the effusions of the Spirit; and also in 1833. A larger number were blessed with revivals in 1834, and no less than eighteen in 1835; and between one and two hundred students were brought hopefully into the kingdom of Christ. It has been estimated that fifteen hundred students were made the hopeful subjects of grace in thirty-six different colleges, from 1820 to 1835 inclusive."

If any thing could make still more apparent the connection between this Concert of Prayer and the frequent revivals of religion that have occurred in our colleges since its appointment, it is the additional fact that these revivals have nearly all occurred during the winter term in which the concert is observed, and for the most part shortly after its observance. That is, perhaps, the most favorable season of the year for special attention to personal religion in colleges, as it is also in churches. There is also no doubt a natural tendency in such a concert to produce such results. When the eyes of the whole church are directed simultaneously towards the young men in our institutions of learning, it would be strange if they did not turn their thoughts towards themselves and each other; and if their teachers did not feel deeply their responsibilities in regard to them, and warn and entreat them tenderly, not only publicly, but in private; and if pious parents and friends did not pray for them, and write to them with peculiar pathos and power,—thus producing a concentration of interest which it would seem must burn upon the most seared conscience, and warm the coldest heart. And God, who loves *united* prayer, and also works by all suitable means, has heard the prayer of his people, and made use of these favorable circumstances, and given efficacy to his Word, which is usually preached with unusual pungency at such times; and the consequence is, that *that Winter Term*, and more especially the last few weeks of it, have been the birth season of hundreds and thousands of young men in college, who are now ministers of the gospel and teachers of youth, and missionaries of the cross and men of influence in every department of life, in almost every portion of the world. Could the concert be observed by all the churches; observed with earnest and believing prayer not only, but also with *fasting* (for this kind goeth not out but with *prayer and fasting*), we might hope for far more glorious results. And if our colleges were also remembered every Sabbath in the prayers of the sanctuary, and every morning and evening in the prayers of pious families,—remembered with that particularity and tenderness, and importunity and faith which their peculiar character and standing demands from the whole church, and which the providence and the Spirit of God have so conspicuously sanctioned and encouraged,—we might hope that the good influence would not only be felt every year, but be diffused and prolonged through the year; thus preventing apostasy and inconsistency, sustaining a more uniform, as well as more elevated standard of piety, and bringing into the ministry whole classes and colleges of such holy men as God could consistently own and bless in the speedy conversion of the whole world to himself.

We cannot conclude this chapter without adverting to some facts, which, at the present time, are fitted to awaken special anxiety, and which conspire with the encouraging circumstances, of which we have spoken, to call for special earnestness in prayer. For a few years past, there has been a serious decline in the number of those who have entered the ministry. The highest numbers furnished by the principal Theological Seminaries in New England and New York in any one year since 1820 was in 1838, when it reached one hundred and sixty-eight. From that time there was a regular decrease, till, in 1843, it fell below one hundred; and with the exception of a single year, it never rose above one hundred between that time and 1850. The number of students connected with the Theological Seminaries of New England alone was one hundred and twenty-five less in 1852 than in 1840.

If we pause a moment to inquire into the causes of this decrease, we shall find in them increased occasion for prayerful solicitude, though the responsibility does not attach solely, or even chiefly, to the colleges. It is *not* owing to a decrease of *college students.* On the contrary, the number of undergraduates in the colleges of New England was greater by two hundred and five in 1852 than in 1840. Moreover, during this period, not a few new colleges have come into active operation in the West and in other parts of the country.

Neither is it because the colleges have ceased to be blessed with special outpourings of the Spirit. On the contrary, in the new colleges of the West, at least, the period of decline now under consideration, and which comprises the larger portion of their history, has been marked by numerous revivals. In addition to those already alluded to, four revivals occurred in Knox College in the space of six years, ending in 1852. A precious work of grace was enjoyed at Illinois College in 1853, and another in the early part of 1854. About the same time, Marietta College was blessed with one of the most powerful revivals known in its history. And in 1852, the revivals in our colleges generally were more numerous and powerful, than in any year since 1820, with the exception of 1831, resulting in the hopeful conversion of not much less than three hundred young men connected with some fifteen institutions.

The decrease of candidates for the ministry may be referred mainly to two general causes; viz., the comparative unfrequency of revivals in the churches, and perhaps, also, in some of the older colleges; and the prevalence of a worldly spirit, turning away young men from the toils and sacrifices of the ministry to the numberless and tempting fields of enterprise that open on every hand. The effect is seen, in the first place, in the unusually small proportion of pious students that are brought into colleges from the churches. In 1832, fifty out of ninety who entered the Freshman Class in Yale College were professedly pious. For two or three years past, pious students have numbered less than one third of the class. Never in the history of Amherst College has a class entered with so small a ratio of professed Christians as the class of 1850, though, it should be added, that there has since been an increase to nearly the usual ratio. In Dartmouth College, the proportion of professors of religion has probably never been smaller than at present; certainly it is much smaller than it was fifteen or twenty years ago.

In the second place, the operation of these causes is seen in the fact, that in most of our colleges, and probably in all, a smaller proportion of pious students enter the ministry than in former years. Probably there is no college in New England, where so large a proportion of the pious students enter the ministry as in Amherst College. Yet in Amherst College, whereas it was formerly a rare thing for a pious young man to engage in any secular calling,—so rare as to occasion remark and surprise,—now it is by no means so rare or remarkable.

We have spoken of these causes as two. The cause, after all, is radically one, namely, the prevalence of a worldly and self-seeking, instead of a self-denying and Christian spirit ; and the remedy is one, namely, larger measures of divine influence. Nothing else will make the churches more reasonable in their demands, and more generous in their treatment of the ministry ; ready, in a word, to remove every needless toil and trial from the sacred office. Nothing else can dispose and prepare unconverted, or even converted young men, whether in the college or in the community, to bear cheerfully the crushing weight of labors and responsibilities that devolve on the ministry under the most favorable circumstances. Only He, who made man, can make an able and faithful minister of the gospel. The residue of the Spirit is with God, and he will bestow it only in answer to the prayers of those who love Zion.

If we turn now from the supply of ministers to the demand for them, we find that while the former has been diminishing, the latter has been constantly and rapidly increasing, in consequence of the vast extension of our national domain, the unparalleled increase of population, the organization of new States and the multiplication of churches, together with the wide fields opened to missionary effort in all parts of the world. Since the annual supply of ministers began to decrease, a million square miles have been added to our national territory, five to the number of States, and seven millions to our population. Emigration has been pouring its hundreds of thousands—enough to form a new State—every year into our country ; and these, for the most part, wedded to one of two great and growing forms of fatal error,—the Celtic races to popery and the Teutonic races to infidelity. The former are establishing colleges and seminaries at every commanding point, and summoning all their energies to gain, through timid or corrupt politicians, the control of our common schools. The latter are holding conventions, lifting up their voice in high places, and seizing on the mighty enginery of the press. And both are, at this moment, marching with unprecedented boldness to possess themselves of the sovereignty in the great cities, both on the Atlantic coast and on the great rivers of the West, threatening to trample down in their march the Bible, the Sabbath and our most sacred institutions. Our field is literally the world. Not only is the world open, and the harvest every where ripe for the labors of foreign missionaries, but all nations, from the Emerald Isle on the West to the Celestial Empire on the East, are flocking to our own shores. Europe looks with mingled wonder and fear on our free institutions, our growing political and moral power; and while despots watch for our fall, the masses wait for our national intervention, or at least look with unutterable hopes and longings for our social, moral and religious influence. Asia and Africa, too, hang on America their chief hopes for knowledge and liberty and eternal life.

The concurrence of these facts, this diminution of supply on the one hand, and increase of demand on the other, has produced an exigency, which is universally acknowledged and felt, and which brings from all our missionary boards, and from all our ecclesiastical organizations, loud and earnest calls for men. Every number of our missionary journals comes laden with the cry, "Give us *men ;* where are the *men* to be found who will carry the bread of life to the millions that are perishing with hunger?" And the cry that thus reaches the readers of these journals, is only a *faint echo* of the many and loud voices that call from the North and the South and the East and the West, "Come over and help us!"

Never was there a time when so many men, and such wise and holy men, were needed for ministers and missionaries, and teachers and rulers, and every other post of influence. Never especially was there a time when there was such an imperative demand for a numerous, learned and godly ministry. Never did such encouragements and such necessities meet and press with such combined force on the consciences and the hearts of all who seek the prosperity of Zion. And at such a time, that there should be a decrease instead of an increase in the number of candidates for the ministry; and when we look from the wasting streams to the fountains, that we should find the supply failing there; that at such a time, revivals should be fewer and less powerful, and the number of professors of religion falling off; and a smaller proportion of these even should be preparing for the ministry, not only in the churches but in the colleges, which were established for the very purpose, above all others, of meeting just this want with a steady and permanent supply;—is it not alarming and deplorable to the last degree? Does it not roll a fearful responsibility on the guardians and teachers, on the patrons and pious students, on ministers and Christians, on all who have any connection with or concern for our colleges or our churches, a fearful responsibility touching the present religious state of these institutions? When the wants of our country and the cries of the struggling nations,—when the church and the world,—when humanity and religion,—when the providence and Word and Spirit of God,—when every thing that can speak and every thing that hath breath, is calling upon our colleges, as with an audible voice, to go forward; to train and send forth the captains who shall lead on the sacramental host of the Lord's anointed to the conquest of the world for learning and piety, for heaven and God,—must there be a backward movement in the very van of the army,—a failure of duty and of resources in the very citadel of the Holy City? Where will the responsibility of such a dereliction fall? or, rather, where will it not fall? Who will be free from a share in the guilt? Who that has any sympathy with Christ can fail to go to him at once, and plead before him the very argument which he himself has put into our mouths: The harvest *truly* is *great*, and the laborers are few; thou Lord of the harvest, send forth laborers into the harvest; and to this end, pour out thy Spirit in speedy and copious effusions on the young men in our colleges, who need only a new heart to fit them for this work; who are already far advanced in their intellectual training, and who alone can be immediately prepared to meet this immediate and pressing necessity. Thou who didst feed the fainting multitudes in the wilderness with the few loaves and the few small fishes, pity the untold multitudes of fainting souls who are ready to perish in the deserts of heathenism,—nay, in the very cities and villages of this Christian land,—to perish for ever, because there is none to break unto them the bread of eternal life.

CHAPTER XII.

Responsibilities of Guardians and Teachers, Pious Students and Pious Parents—Trustees—The Legislative Power—Charge of Funds—General Oversight—A Religious Society—Responsibility for the Religious State of Colleges—Power of Appointment—Duty to appoint Christian Teachers—Faculty—The Executive Power—Immediate Charge and Principal Responsibility—Scholars—Christians—Opportunities for Christian Influence—Recitations—Prayers—Dr. Dwight—Preaching—Revivals—Personal Conversation with Students—Prayer—Due to Themselves, to their Pupils, to the Design and History of Colleges, to the Church, to Mankind and to God—Pious Students—Some Advantages even over the Officers—Example—Power to do Evil—Power to do Good—Brainerd—Taylor—True Distinction-Pious Parents—Influence over Sons in Vacation—Power of Prayer—Facts—Revival in Amherst College—Converts subjects of Special Prayer—Children of the Covenant.

THE responsibility for our colleges rests primarily on those who have the charge of them. These are the trustees and the faculty, who are invested the one with the legislative, the other with the executive power. The former control the funds, enact the laws, and appoint the teachers; the latter execute the laws, administer the government, and impart the instruction.

The trustees are the sole legal representatives of the college. In law, therefore, and in the eye of the State, the sole responsibility is theirs. And the highest *moral* responsibility devolves *ultimately* on those who have the supreme power.

The trustees are invested with the exclusive disposal of the funds. It is their duty, therefore, to see that these funds be neither wasted nor perverted; that they be faithfully applied, if special donations, to the purpose for which they were originally given, or, if general funds, to the object for which the college was established. This is not a responsibility to be lightly esteemed, or carelessly undertaken, especially as our colleges grow older and richer, and, as with the lapse of time, the sacred purpose for which most of them were founded is liable to be forgotten, or overlooked. Such a trust can be properly discharged only by men of enlightened minds and tender consciences, familiar with the history of American colleges, and imbued with the spirit of their pious founders ; skilled in the management of funds, and scrupulously upright in the administration of them ; men who will study and carry out the intentions of the fathers, or founders, with the same sacred honor and integrity with which they would execute the last will and testament of a beloved friend ; who will watch over the interests of the institution committed to their care with all, and more than all, the wakeful solicitude with which they would cherish the welfare of orphan children commended to their guardianship by the last accents of parental love. The colleges *are* the adopted children of "parents passed into the skies," and the trustees are their guardians.

The trustees are charged with the general oversight of colleges. They are, therefore, properly responsible for its general character and state, whether as it regards literature, morals or religion. To this end, they must be qualified to judge of all those great interests ; and not only competent, but disposed to devise suitable ways and means for their advancement

They should be intelligent men—themselves, for the most part, of collegiate education; acquainted by personal experience, not only with literature and science, but with college life. They should be Christian men, men of experimental piety and Christian benevolence; who will give religion that first place in their hearts, and, so far as in them lies, in the institution, to which it is, in its own nature, entitled, and which it has received in all the early history of American colleges. The college is, in its origin, essentially a religious institution; and it is the first duty, the paramount obligation of the trustees, to see that it answers, in this respect, its original intention. The trustees of Yale College early claimed that colleges are, in their nature, religious societies; that the corporation, as the head of such a society, are so far forth an ecclesiastical body; and accordingly, by their own authority, they constituted the first church in the college, and installed the professor of divinity its first pastor. Whatever may be thought of such a claim, the trustees of our colleges are certainly bound, in view of such facts, to feel a peculiar responsibility for the religious character of the institutions under their care; to *know* what their religious state is, and see that it is what it should be, so far as their corporate action can make and keep it so. Above all, it is incumbent on them to watch and pray, that nothing be suffered to hinder or impair those divine influences, which have been the prosperity and glory of American colleges, and which, from these fountains, have flowed in such copious streams over the American churches and the American people.

Unless they come up to this standard, we see not how they can be morally guiltless of a serious breach of trust.

But it is in the exercise of the appointing power, that the trustees exert the most direct and decisive influence over the college. And this brings us to the consideration of the collateral question, what sort of men should compose the faculty, on whom devolves the immediate government and instruction.

They must of course be learned men, disciplined in mind, cultivated in taste, thoroughly trained in all the branches of literature and science, and especially masters of the department to which they devote themselves; apt to teach also, sound in their principles, correct in their habits; so far as possible, model teachers and model men. This is a thing of such obvious and acknowledged necessity, that it will be looked to as a matter of course. An instructor in college without distinguished literary attainments and an unblemished moral character, would be immediately pronounced unfit for his office; and the college, whose president and professors should be deficient in these intellectual and moral qualifications, would soon be destitute also of pupils and patrons.

But is their religious character and influence less important? Is religion so unimportant in itself, and so irrelevant to the design of a college, that genuine piety should not be deemed an essential qualification of a college officer; that he should be appointed to the office without once raising the question, whether he is a Christian, and be suffered to make his mark on hundreds of leading minds, hundreds of immortal spirits, without any inquiry whether it is a Christian impress ? Not in a Christian country, which owes its unexampled prosperity to the Christian religion. Not by the Christian church, whose members hang all their hopes for this life and the next on that religion. Not in Christian colleges, which were founded by holy men chiefly for sacred purposes.

The officers of college may be all that we have above supposed, in their intellectual and moral qualifications, and yet be radically unfit for their office. They must be Christians, and that not merely by profession and creed, but practically, experimentally, heartily Christian ; eminently holy and devoted men, full of love to Christ and all for whom Christ died,—whose hearts shall be in lively sympathy with revivals, Christian missions, and every enterprise of benevolence ; and whose learning, all baptized in a purer fount, shall all be consecrated to the cause of charity, humanity and God. The want of such a Christian spirit is, in reality, and should be esteemed, a disqualification for the office, less glaring perhaps, but not less essential and fatal, than the want of learning or the want of a good moral character. We are well aware that when religious considerations are allowed to interfere with the claims of a candidate otherwise well qualified for a professorship, there are always enough to raise the cry of "sectarianism," "proscription," "religious test," &c. But if we have taken the right view of the design and history of American colleges, religious considerations ought to have, not only some, but paramount influence in such appointments. Few, if any, of those who make the outcry against "religious tests," would exclude them altogether. Would *they* consider a Hume or a Gibbon a suitable candidate for the historical professorship in an English university or an American college ? But why not ? He would probably distance all competitors in his mastery of the facts and the philosophy of history. Would *they* be accessory to the appointment of a Voltaire or a Condorcet to the chair of ethical and political philosophy ? But why not ? These were men of brilliant talents and vast erudition. Why then complain, if the trustees of a college founded by Christian men, and primarily for a Christian object, should refuse to elect to the professorship of Natural Science, or of Ancient Languages,—to say nothing of Divinity,—a man, however well qualified in other respects, who can see no footsteps of a personal Creator in the material universe, or who can find no traces of a divine Redeemer in the Scriptures ? The truth is, our colleges are foundations "sacred to Christ and his church," and to place upon them an incumbent who does not hold the truth and the Spirit of Christ, is to desecrate them. They are religious institutions, and to secularize them is to pervert them. So it would have seemed in the eyes of the founders ; and men who will not exercise the responsible functions of the appointing power on the same principles, have no right to accept the office of trustee in such institutions.

We are now prepared to consider the duties and responsibilities of the faculty. Supposing them to be such men as we have described, what opportunities will they have for exerting a Christian influence?

As officers of instruction, they come in direct daily contact with the students; and every day will bring with it some opportunity of saying or doing something that will have an important bearing on their religious character and their eternal destiny. It will be of very little use for them to lug in their preaching or their moralizing as a matter of official duty, when they have no heart for the work. But if the heart is ever full of Christian truth, and ever warm with holy love, it will not want frequent opportunities to pour itself out in those words spoken in season, which are like apples of gold in pictures of silver.

The daily studies of the class-room will often suggest a religious lesson, that may be dropped by the way. The classic author may illustrate by resemblance or by contrast the doctrine or the language of the sacred page. The scientific treatise may raise the thoughts to the infinite Author of all science. The weekly Bible exercise, which, we are happy to know, exists in so many colleges, affords an opportunity of rendering learning subservient to religion; which the Christian teacher will seize with avidity, and improve with a zeal tempered by wisdom,—which will be remembered, and remembered with respect and pleasure by his pupils, perhaps long after he has ceased from his labors. The morning and evening prayer, formal and heartless as it sometimes is, need not be so, and will not be so, if the officers, as in turn they officiate at the altar, will give it their thoughts, and prepare their hearts for it, as they prepare their minds for the daily lessons, and throw their whole souls into it at all times, as they sometimes do in seasons of special religious interest. Such prayers as Dr. Dwight poured forth in the chapel of Yale College, when in the agony of his spirit he wrestled with God, as well as struggled with men for the victory over error and sin—such prayers as we have heard, all the year round, and year after year, from the honored and beloved president of Amherst College—such prayers never fall powerless on the ear of man or God; never fail to carry the whole assembly of worshippers, with a wise and sacred violence, into the very presence of their Maker.

Many college officers are also preachers of the gospel. It is desirable that they should be. There is no better discipline for the mind, as well as the heart of the teacher, than the study of theology. The sacred science is the centre of all the other sciences, and the Sacred Writings are the fountain of a literature that is higher, richer, purer than any other. It is well in many respects (though not perhaps best in every respect) that the professors should all take part in the preaching to the students on the Sabbath. It turns their attention to the spiritual interests of their pupils, and obliges them all to share directly in the responsibility, as of their literary proficiency, so of their immortal well-being. Here, again, complaint is often made of the college chapel as containing the worst possible audience for preachers. But the fault is in the preachers more than in the hearers. Good preachers find good audiences every where, and nowhere better than in the college chapel. The college is the last place in the world to go to with scientific dissertations, or literary essays, or poetical prettinesses. Such sermons will of course raise an army of critics, like the sowing of dragons' teeth. But manly, truthful and earnest appeals to their understanding, their consciences and their hearts, students will hear, will respect, will feel, will remember, will profit by, as surely and as abundantly as any audience in Christendom. The opportunity to preach to such an audience is a sacred privilege, which the college officer cannot too highly prize ; a priceless talent, for the improvement of which he must give a solemn account.

Revivals of religion should be an object of special prayer and labor with the officers of colleges. Revivals are so adapted, as we have already said, to the nature and relations of young men in college, that there is very little hope of maintaining in them even an ordinary standard of piety and a tolerable state of religion, without frequent seasons of special religious interest ; and these cannot be expected to occur unless they are specially contemplated, earnestly desired, confidently expected, and perseveringly sought by suitable prayer and effort. A revival every four years is the very lowest standard that will meet at all the necessities of the case, that every class, at least, may reap the fruits of one of those hallowed seasons. A revival every year is what is manifestly needed to bring every class at once under the controlling influence of religious principle, and to keep the standard high and rising from the beginning to the end of the course. And we do believe if the officers of college would plan for it, and toil for it, and pray for it, and look for it, as they do for other and inferior ends ; and if the united prayers of the church might also go up for it, this exceedingly desirable result might be attained. "Be it unto thee according to thy faith," is the language which the providence and the Spirit, as well as the Word of God, utters almost with an audible voice to all who seek his face, but most emphatically to those who watch and pray for the spiritual welfare of students in college. It were good *economy* in the government of the students to labor for frequent revivals. Such a college, as we have described, would govern itself. There is no dissipation, no vice, no call for discipline, in time of revival, and for some time after. The presence of God is too visible, too awful for such profanation. The moral power of truth and holiness is too clearly seen and too deeply felt. Let such seasons become so frequent that their influence shall continue, and, so to speak, overlap each other, and the college will be an easily governed community, well ordered and beautiful in itself, as well as a school of discipline and preparation for heaven.

Personal conversation of the officers with the students on the subject of personal religion is an important means of good, not only in revivals, but at all seasons. Why should students go away from Christian colleges, where the teachers are all, or nearly all, professed Christians, and many of them Christian ministers, and where revivals occur every few years, and complain that not one of those teachers has ever said a word to them personally on that great subject, which is the chief concern of every human being, which is the most essential element in every student's education?

Direct intercourse and intercommunion of officers with students is much more frequent now than it was in the days of our fathers, when students must take off their hats if they came in sight of a college officer; and when, of course, they shunned the sight of an officer, as the children and youth of the parish, for a similar reason, dreaded the visits of the parson. The consequence is (and this is one of the most encouraging aspects of the times in regard to colleges), that the faculty and the students no longer constitute two parties, as they then did, with opposing interests and hostile feelings. It is a great safeguard to *individual* students, also, to feel that this and that officer cherish a personal regard for them. Nothing makes a young man more reckless than to feel that he has no *friends* in the community where he dwells; none to care for him, none to be specially gratified if he does well, and none to be deeply grieved if he acts an unworthy part.

In one college, where perhaps personal intercourse is carried as far, or farther, than in any other, there is no member of college who is not invited to the house of some officer every year in his college course. Visits to students at their rooms, also, are not mere formal calls of police officers to spy out their quarters, but, often at least, friendly visits and pleasant conversations, which not unfrequently take a religious turn. Some system is also observed in these visits and conversations, and such a division of labor is made as to extend them to all the students. The result is believed to be most happy, not only in the religious state of the college, but in its government, and in all the relations of officers and students. And the only regret of the officers is, that they do not find more time for such intercourse, and have not the heart to turn it oftener to a good religious account.

Above all, college officers should be men of prayer, above other *men*, for they hold a post of greater responsibility than most ; above all other *things*, for prayer is the most important of all their duties, and, in some sense, comprehensive of all. For to pray well is not only to study well, as the Reformers thought, but to teach well and preach well, and govern well and guide well the minds and hearts intrusted to their charge. Every public *exercise*, literary as well as religious, should be preceded by prayer, as much as those of a pastor, and for the same reason ; every such exercise is forming characters for time and for eternity, and, if guided by wisdom and blessed by grace from on high, may contribute much to form them for usefulness here and happiness hereafter. Every *place*—the study, the recitation-room, the laboratory and the library, not less than the closet and the chapel—should be baptized with prayer. They should pray not only for the whole college, but for classes, and sections and individuals. This will awaken increased interest in such individuals, and not only secure greater faithfulness, but lead naturally to a more felicitous use of all suitable opportunities and means for doing them good. They should *watch* for *souls*, and pray with and for them as those that must *give account*; for never had any class of men greater facilities for doing this with such a reasonable prospect of a happy result than college officers: and they cannot escape the responsibility of using or neglecting the ten talents that are thus put into their hands. They owe it to themselves, for nothing will so fit them for the best performance of their literary as well as their religious duties; nothing will contribute so much to their honor and happiness here, or make them shine so brightly as stars of the first magnitude in the firmament for ever. They owe it to their character as Christian men; to their profession, many of them, as Christian ministers, and to their office as Christian teachers in Christian institutions. They owe it to their pupils, who look to their instructions and example as an illustration of what is most worthy to be pursued; and to the parents of those pupils, who, in intrusting them to their care, wish them to be taught, first of all, the things that are most excellent, and who desire nothing so much as that their children may be found walking in the truth. They owe it to the college system, which was chiefly intended for religious purposes; to the history of American colleges, which has been to so great an extent a history of the labors of wise and good men, owned and blessed by the providence and grace of God; to the halls and rooms which they occupy, or visit, and the very ground on which they tread,—all of which have been hallowed by the prayers of ministers and missionaries, and holy men, and by the more sacred presence of the Divine Spirit. Are there not some rooms in all our colleges, and all the rooms in some of them, where the stone would cry out of the wall at the profanation, and the beam out of the timber would answer it, if they were ever desecrated to unholy revelry, or even to mere secular pursuits and selfish gratifications? They owe it to the church, which looks to them for a learned and godly ministry; to the Commonwealth and the country, which depend on them for wise and pious rulers; to the present age, which hangs on its educated men its only earthly hope of deliverance from the peculiar errors and dangers by which it is beset; to the cause of truth and righteousness, and liberty and humanity, which will roll on in safety to complete triumph, or be stopped in its victorious career, or be thrown off the safe track, according to the wisdom or the folly, the faithfulness or the unfaithfulness, of those engineers and conductors who are now under the training of the officers of college. They owe it to mankind, whose destinies, for time and eternity, are intrusted, under God, in so large a measure to their keeping. They owe it, above all, to God, whose they are and whom they serve, who has put them in this high post of trust and influence, and endowed them with the qualifications for it; who, by his wonder-working providence, has thrown the whole educational system so entirely into the hands of Christian men and Christian ministers; and who, in his more wonderful grace, has shown so much readiness to cooperate with them by his Spirit in the discharge of their responsible duties. They stand on holy ground, and the Lord, out of the burning bush, calls on them to put their shoes from off their feet, and receive, with holy awe and obedient will, his commission for the redemption of his chosen people. They stand at the fountain-head, and all who dwell along the banks, or drink from the waters, will hold them responsible for the streams. They possess the citadel in the city of God, and earth and heaven expect them to do their duty.

In conclusion of this chapter, we cannot but advert to the concurrent responsibility of pious students in college, and also of pious parents and friends. In some respects, pious students have the advantage, even over the officers, in opportunities of doing good to their fellow-students, as individuals. They are on the same level with those whom they would benefit, and in constant contact with them. Like the professedly pious brothers and sisters in a family, their *example* has even more power, perhaps, than that of the parents. They are literally known and read by the whole community, and whether they will or not, they cannot but exert an influence. The unchristian life of one professor of religion may raise doubts in many a mind, as to the reality of experimental piety. On the other hand, the silent example of one manifestly sincere, consistent, every-day Christian, has been like an anchor, that has held many a doubting and tempest-tossed soul around him to a belief of the truth as it is in Jesus. We shudder when we remember the incalculable mischief that has been done by a talented and accomplished, but ungodly youth, as he has gone through college scattering firebrands, arrows and death, while other young minds, as inflammable as gunpowder, stand thick around him. Again, it thrills us with delight to recall the career of one and another young man of remarkable piety, whose heart was full of love to the souls of men, whose closet burned with a perpetual fire on the altar, whose room, at all times a Bethel, became, in seasons of revival, emphatically the house of God and the gate of heaven ; whose lips, always ready to speak for Christ and his cause, at such seasons overflowed with impassioned and resistless eloquence ; and whose life, a pattern of faithfulness in every duty, was clothed with marvellous power to persuade men and to please God. Many a revival in college has seemed to turn on the influence of *one* such pious student. What power would there not be then in a college church *made up* of such young Christians ? What Freshman Class could withstand the power of such a church, when it first came under their influence ? Oh, how can Christian students come into the places and occupy the rooms of such men—men, who in college, like David Brainerd and James Brainerd Taylor, and many others whom we have known, have turned many to righteousness—without seeing and feeling deeply that here is a distinction far above ordinary college distinctions, far above all worldly greatness, to shine like them in usefulness on earth and in glory above the stars ? Alas ! that such a field of usefulness should be overlooked by so many young men who might do more good in it than most men do in all their lives ; and at the same time, by the very process of cultivating it, might most effectually prepare themselves for further labor in whatever field the Lord of the harvest may assign them. What more beautiful spectacle can there be on earth, than *youth* devoted to *God*, and *learning* joined in holy wedlock to *religion!* And what study can there be more worthy of a Christian student than to consummate such a union!

Pious parents, while they labor for the conversion or the increasing sanctification of their own sons, may, and do, exert no inconsiderable influence on the religious state of college. Their personal influence on their sons during the vacation may have an important bearing not only on their character, but also on the salvation of others; may thwart all the good influences of the previous term, or may seal all the literary and social, as well as moral and religious impressions, which faithful teachers are at so much pains to make. The letters of a godly mother or a pious sister, freighted with wisdom and love, are fraught also with moral power to touch and soften the hardest heart, and thence often to reach the hearts of others.

But the chief reliance of pious friends at a distance must be on the power of prayer. However separated by distance, they can meet their sons, if pious, every morning and evening at a common mercy-seat; and if not pious, they can reach them at any time through a presence which they cannot escape, and a power which they cannot resist; not only meet, or reach them, but lay their hands, as it were, upon them, and leave a blessing on their heads. What an unspeakable privilege! What a blessed medium of approach and influence over those far away! Nor is this fancy or enthusiasm. Facts go beyond imagination in regard to this very power, as it has been exerted on the members of college, especially in times of revival. After one of those happy seasons, of which there have been so many at Amherst College, President Hitchcock addressed a letter to the parents of the converts, and found to his surprise (no, we will not say *surprise*, for he seems to have expected it, but to his wonder and delight) that in a majority of cases parents and friends at home had felt an unusual solicitude for these very youth. Even though they had heard nothing of *their* state of mind, and knew nothing of the state of religious feeling in college, still they were waiting with unutterable longings, or with confident expectations, to hear of the conversion of their impenitent children.

Another very interesting fact, which was developed in this revival, and which has been found to be equally true of many others, is, that a very large proportion of the converts were "children of the covenant;" a fact full of encouragement to parents, who dedicate their children from infancy to the Lord in the ordinance of baptism, but which also illustrates forcibly the responsibility of parents for the salvation of their children. Of 63 who were admitted to the church in Yale College, as fruits of the revival of 1802, all but eight were "children of the covenant." Of 22 who were received to the communion after that of 1808, every individual had been baptized in infancy; and of 70 who professed religion after the revival of 1831, all but ten were the children of pious parents. If pious parents would but watch for the souls of their sons in college as they care and toil for their worldly prosperity; if the church would but do her duty to the *baptized children* of the church, who are members of college, what a redeeming and sanctifying element would, by this means alone, be infused into our literary institutions! But we must devote another chapter to the responsibility of the church and its ministers.

CHAPTER XIII.

Duty of the Church and the Ministry to the Colleges—The Church the Mother of the Colleges—The Ministers their Sons in a double sense—Not Secular Institutions—Western College Society—Paramount Duty of Ministers to root Colleges in the Confidence of the Churches and the Common People—College Foundations—The Young Men of the Church—A Blessing to the Churches to educate them—Southampton, Westhampton—True idea of an Education Society—Comprehensive—The Whole Cause one—A Fundamental Object—Large Funds necessity for Charitable Aid—The Prayers of the Church—A Treasure laid up in Heaven—Cannot be squandered or perverted.

The church cannot roll off all responsibility for the religious state of colleges upon college officers. She could not, if she would; and we are sure she would not, if she could. She is the mother of the colleges, and she cannot but endow them with more or less of her property, and follow them with her blessing and her prayers. And the ministers in turn are (many of them in a double sense) the sons of the colleges. Most of them received their education there; very many of them were spiritually born there.

The impression has sometimes prevailed (though the providence of God and the remonstrances of enlightened men have done much of late to remove that impression), that colleges are secular institutions, and, as such, have no special claim on the charities or the prayers of the church. But they were not so esteemed by our Pilgrim Fathers, who planted Harvard College in the midst of the churches, and watered it with their prayers and tears; and lavished on it their treasures too,—the riches of their poverty and liberality,—as they gave for no other object of Christian charity. They were not so considered by those ministers who endowed Yale College with the choicest gifts from their libraries, and, in that very act, consecrated a perpetual union between learning and religion. They were not so viewed by those who, with pious and, for the most part, clerical hands, founded the College of New Jersey and Dartmouth College, and the other institutions that sprung up in all sections of the country during the transition period, in which the political power was passing from the Mother Country to the Colonies and the United States. They have not been so regarded by those wise and holy men who have built so many colleges in the old and the new States during the last quarter of a century. The whole history of colleges proves that they have not been, and were never intended to be, secular institutions. They always have been Christian schools,—a sort of religious society; and if they are to live and prosper, they must still continue to enjoy the patronage and the prayers, they must still be more or less directly under the watch and care of the Christian church and the Christian ministry. The Western College Society has done good service in bringing this question distinctly before the Christian public, and establishing this principle on the solid basis of historical facts and incontrovertible arguments; and this Society is as strictly a religious society, and as well entitled to be heard from the pulpit on the Sabbath, and to share in the subscriptions of the church, or the contributions of the sanctuary, as the Education Society, the Tract Society, or the Missionary Society itself. The institutions which it represents are in no small measure the executive power and active agency,—the controlling head and the laboring hand of them all. All the money that can be poured into the treasuries of these societies is worthless and powerless, unless the colleges furnish the men. And ministers of the gospel could hardly render a more important service to the churches and the cause of benevolence at this moment than by preaching, in connection with the claims of this Society, or at their pleasure, on the indissoluble connection between the pecuniary, literary and religious condition of colleges and the permanent prosperity of the churches. Ministers, as educated men, see the mutual relations of learning and religion more clearly, and feel them more deeply, than the great majority of their people can. But by instructing them, line upon line, on the subject, they may bring their people up to some near approximation to their own just conceptions. And this is the paramount duty which the clergy owe to the higher seminaries of learning; to endeavor to wipe away from them the twofold prejudice, that they are secular establishments, on the one hand, and on the other, that they are aristocratic institutions; and so to root them in the confidence of Christians and the common people, that no heresiarch or demagogue can ever again hope to gain popularity, or even toleration, in assailing them.

There is a select, but growing class of church members, whose wealth, combined with intelligence and liberality, fits them peculiarly to be the patrons of literary institutions,—by the endowment of professorships, the building of libraries, the establishment of prizes and other foundations, which shall furnish the *material* of education for this and future generations. It requires more than ordinary faith, or sagacity and mental enlargement, to found and endow colleges for generations yet unborn, as it does to establish political institutions, or plant orchards and shade-trees, for the benefit of after ages. But such men live when others die and are forgotten; live in the good they do, and in the memory of a grateful posterity. If any man is to be envied, it is he who has the *means* and the *heart* thus to enlarge and perpetuate fountains of holy influence in a dark and sinful world; who will teach and preach in all coming ages through an uninterrupted series of learned and pious professors, or speak to the leading minds of many generations from the books, and the very shelves and walls of a college library,—"that shrine where," as Lord Bacon says, "all the relics of the ancient saints, full of true virtue, and without delusion or imposture, are preserved and reposed."

It is not men of large wealth only, however, who may enjoy the luxury of doing good permanently,—of perpetuating their influence through college endowments. Men in ordinary circumstances can combine to found a scholarship. A church can fill an alcove, and a Christian, of no great resources, can fill a shelf in the library. An association or presbytery can endow a professorship. A denomination can rear an academy or a college in some new section, where nothing but corn or cotton would grow of itself for many a year, but where it will soon be needed; and the very sight of it will help to make Christian scholars and Christian ministers.

But the churches can contribute to the colleges a richer gift than money. They can send to them their sons, especially their pious sons, to be educated for the gospel ministry; those church members who have the ability, educating their own sons, and *taking pains* to educate them for this self-denying work, instead of taking pains to keep them at home that they may make money; and the church, as a body, seeking out their young men who are poor, but pious and promising, and encouraging and aiding them not to look for the easiest or the fattest place, but, at whatever sacrifice of worldly prospects, to prepare themselves for future usefulness by a public education. In so doing, as benevolence is always twice blessed, they would bless the college and bless themselves.

A college can have no more desirable members, no more useful element introduced into it, than young men of this class. They aid in its *government* by their good example. They teach lessons scarcely less valuable, and with scarcely less power, than those which are inculcated from the professor's chair. Their habits of industry, economy, fidelity and piety speak, with more than the eloquence of words, to every eye that sees them, and act upon the whole community like the little leaven, that leavens the whole lump.

The church, in turn, is blessed in the very self-denial of parting with them, in the very act of seeking them out and setting them on towards a higher sphere of duty and usefulness; in the whole process of encouraging and sustaining them while they get their education. It is blessed, also, in the reflex influence which they exert upon it, as they return, from term to term, with enlarging powers and increasing knowledge and growing piety, to mingle with them at their homes and firesides; to aid them in their meetings for prayer and conference, and to give new life to education, temperance, revivals, missions and every good cause. Such a connecting link between a Christian church and a truly Christian college is often an unspeakable blessing to that church and the whole community. And as, in the course of time, several such men go forth from the same church, and settle in the ministry, or engage in teaching, or labor in enterprises of charity and benevolence, they become links not only between the church and the college, but between that church and not a few other fountains of good influence, which not only water their own field, or valley, but, like all "the streams of love," "flow back where they begin."

This is a point which demands attention in our day. We are in danger of depending too exclusively on those great societies which constitute the machinery of benevolence; and when we have contributed to them, we are apt to think our duty is done. It is not enough to contribute to the funds of an Education Society—indeed it is of no *use* to contribute to them—unless men can be found, or furnished, for the society to educate. And if this first point is to be overlooked, our Education Societies will soon have no material to work upon, and our Missionary Societies no men to work with, and our colleges must do the best they can with unconverted students, and our churches, for aught we can see, must take up with unconverted ministers, or no ministers at all.

Where is the church, that will again set the example, and where are the churches that will follow the example, which was so well set in former times by the churches in Southampton and Westhampton, but which, we fear, is not now very well followed even there ; and make a business, not of manufacturing cotton fabrics, but of manufacturing something better—educated men, and ministers of the gospel? Such a community would be intelligent, virtuous and prosperous, by the natural reaction of its educational and benevolent enterprises. Such a community would deserve a premium far higher than was ever awarded at any "World's Fair," and they would *get* it at a vastly grander exhibition, which will one day be made when the inhabitants of more than *one* "world" will be assembled, and a more than royal personage will preside at the distribution of more than royal prizes.

But over and above all private efforts of individual Christians and separate churches, there seems to be a necessity for some public association, which shall take its place among the other accredited representatives of the cause of benevolence, which shall periodically present the *whole subject* of collegiate education, and especially education for the ministry, to the consideration and support of the *whole church* ; and systematically apply their contributions where they are most needed, and will most effectually subserve the cause. Associated effort is the order of the day, and union is strength. Every benevolent object now has its society to represent it, and to watch over its interests. And surely none can be more important, none more indispensable, than collegiate education, especially as related to the Christian ministry. It is essential to the success of all the others, as the means are indispensable to the accomplishment of the end—as the laborers are necessary to the ingathering of the harvest. It underlies all the others, as the foundation underlies and supports the superstructure. Unless this go forward, all other enterprises of Christian benevolence are at a stand, since money and means, of whatever kind, and to whatever amount, are powerless without men.

It is a cause not only of fundamental importance, but of great magnitude ; wide in its bearings, far-reaching in its results, requiring much wisdom in its management, and vast resources for the achievement of its ends. Few have any just conception of the whole expense of collegiate education, and that for the simple reason, that all our colleges afford it for half, or less than half its actual cost ; in other words, collegiate education is from one half to three quarters gratuitous. If the students were charged the whole cost, including grounds, buildings, libraries and apparatus, as well as the support of the officers and other current expenses, tuition would be swelled to so enormous a figure, as to exclude all but the sons of the most wealthy, and quite to appal even them. If, on the other hand, tuition could be entirely free in all our colleges, the privileges of a public education would be brought within the reach of not a few, who now feel themselves to be precluded. If provision were still further made, by scholarships, and prizes at the disposal of the colleges, for the *entire necessary expenses* of all truly meritorious and highly promising young men who desire a collegiate education, the benefits would be still more widely extended, and they would not be confined to the individuals, but would be felt in every nook and corner of society. If these scholarships were not expressly limited in their application to candidates for the ministry, they would tend to increase the number of ministers, since we might hope, that many of the incumbents, if not pious when placed upon the foundation, would become so during their education. Many and many a young man have we known, who longed for an education, but knew no way to secure the cherished desire of his heart, because there are no charitable foundations in most of our colleges, except for pious young men who are preparing for the ministry. Many such become discouraged, turn aside to some more accessible walk of life, and are lost to learning, lost to all hope of preaching the gospel. Others struggle along through poverty and difficulty, and by the providence and grace of God, despite the neglect of men, find their way into the ministry at last, though too often with bodily health and mental education both impaired by their excessive exertions. The colleges should be provided with the means of educating such young men. Still more important is it, that they should be more amply furnished with the means of aiding indigent and pious young men in an education expressly for the ministry; for scholarships, prizes and appropriations within the gift of the *college* are more acceptable to the young men than any other form of charitable aid, and it is believed may be made to exert quite as elevating an influence on the character and attainments.

And this cause, we cannot but add, is *one.* Whether it builds new colleges in the far West, or adds to the educational facilities in the older colleges of the East,—whether it founds libraries or endows professorships, or establishes scholarships or distributes the charities of the churches in direct appropriations to beneficiaries,—it is one and the same sacred enterprise, seeking, though in different ways, the same high and holy end. The American Education Society has done a noble work in having, to so large an extent, for a long course of years supplied the deficiency of charitable foundations in our colleges designed for the benefit of young men having the ministry in view. This aid, as supplemental to what could be received—by means of college endowments—in the shape of reduced cost of instruction, was indispensable to these young men in order to the completion of a thorough course of study. Blot out the history of that Society, and you put out the light in the candlestick of one third of our churches—send back to the farm, or the shop or the counter, one third of those self-denying men who are making the Western wilderness bud and blossom as the rose—and call home one third of those who have planted the banner of the cross on distant heathen shores. And you cast a still darker cloud over the future ; for at this moment, *one half* of those who are preparing to enter the ministerial and the missionary work in our principal theological seminaries, are known to be beneficiaries of the Education Society. We believe that the golden age of the educational enterprise, in its *largest sense,* is yet to come ; that educational facilities will yet be multiplied a hundredfold, and that a *far better education* will be afforded to a *far greater number* of needy and worthy candidates for the ministry in years to come, than have ever been educated in any former year of the history of the church. The discussion of the question, whether the requisite provisions for this work shall be made through separate and independent organizations, or through a single one, so comprehensive in its object as to embrace within its scope all that is essential, *directly* or *indirectly,* to the best possible education of the greatest possible number of able and faithful ministers of the gospel, comes not within the scope of this Essay. It is alike true, that just in proportion as permanent provisions are secured, the necessity for those which are temporary is diminished, and that, in proportion as permanent provisions fail to meet the demands of the church, the urgency of motive to provide temporary supplies is increased.

The agency which the American Education Society had in establishing the Concert of Prayer for colleges, deserves a very high place in the list of its beneficent operations. It has done a blessed work in calling the attention of the churches, from year to year, to the importance of revivals in seminaries of learning. And its influence has been eminently salutary in securing the resort to such institutions of large numbers of youth already pious. This is *auxiliary* influence of great value and power. But it is questionable, after all, whether undue reliance has not been placed upon this temporary and negative, or, at most, partial and inadequate plan of correcting evil at our colleges, as if the most that could be done was to purify streams flowing from fountains *necessarily corrupt.* The true and great idea undoubtedly is to have all arrangements and appointments such that, with God's blessing, the *fountains themselves* may be kept pure, and consequently in all their outflowings carry a holy and happy influence over society. This idea should never be forgotten by the friends of learning and religion. It should be kept ever present, ever prominent in the view of the churches and their ministers. And in all the various ways both of separate and associated action of which we have already spoken,—by giving their money and by giving their best young men,—they may contribute not a little to a consummation so devoutly to be wished.

But there is a still richer gift with which the feeblest church, or the poorest Christian, can endow a college; and which is, after all, a more precious legacy than princely affluence can bestow. It is the legacy of their prayers. The vast funds of Harvard College have been perverted to the propagation of errors which the godly founders of the college would have contemplated with utter abhorrence. But their *prayers* are a fund, intrusted to no human keeping, which can neither be squandered nor perverted; and these prayers, we believe, will yet bring back the recreant child, with her rich dowry, to the faith of the Fathers. Amherst College was passing rich in the faith and prayers of its pious founders, even while it was struggling with poverty; and now it may be doubted whether she is not richer in the prayers of a Graves than in the munificence of a Williston.

There is a foundation in Amherst College given on such terms, that one *half* of the income is *liable* to be called for from year to year, in all coming time, by the *founder* or his *representative*. It is a noble foundation for the college, while, at the same time, it is perhaps a surer provision for the future emergencies of *his own family*, than the wealth and sagacity of one of "the solid men of Boston" could in any other way establish. Even such a foundation may we all establish by our prayers for colleges; a firm foundation for the permanent prosperity of those institutions, and, at the same time, a sure provision for ourselves and our children after us, laid up in God's treasury against the wants and evils that we know not how soon may come upon us, or upon those who are near and dear to us.

A "treasure" of prayers, "laid up in heaven!" that is the true riches for ourselves,—that is the best inheritance for our children,—that is extensive power and enduring influence in the church and the world! It will last as long as the throne of God shall endure; it will have influence with him who inhabits eternity, and governs the universe. Who that has any enlightened self-love, any intelligent regard for his own children and children's children,—any benevolent or prudent forecast for the well-being of posterity,—who that has the opportunity, will not make an investment which is so easily made, and yet promises such sure and rich returns? And who that has any right understanding of the inseparable connection between learning and religion, and the indispensable necessity of Christian colleges to all the great interests of the church and the State, the country and the world, time and eternity; who that believes knowledge to be power,—power to do good on the largest scale, but power also to do evil beyond all calculation; who that has any rational love of country or commonwealth, of mankind or God,—will not do all that prayer can do to lay broad and deep in the education of all classes, but especially of the leading minds in society, the foundations of these many and various interests?

CHAPTER XIV.

Recapitulation—Motives to Prayer in General—Prayer for Colleges—Time and Manner of Prayer.

WHAT an accumulation of various and weighty motives presses upon us; enough, it would seem, to induce *every* man to pray for every right and desirable object; enough, especially, to constrain every American Christian to pray for American colleges! Let us recapitulate the leading considerations, which have been urged in the foregoing chapters, that we may bring their collected force to bear upon our consciences and our hearts.

1. Inducements to prayer in general.

Prayer is a duty. Our nature prompts and impels us to pray. Our circumstances command and invite us to pray. Pagans and Mohammedans would rise up against us, and condemn us, if we did not pray. The Bible commands, exhorts, and entreats us to pray. Patriarchs, prophets and apostles were men of prayer; and our Lord himself taught us both by precept and example to live a life of prayer. The Holy Spirit teaches us to pray, and makes intercession for us, exciting within us emotions that cannot be repressed, and yet cannot be fully uttered. We owe it to our Heavenly Father, who waits to receive our requests. We owe it to our divine Redeemer, who has opened the door of access, and stands ready to introduce us. We owe it to our gracious Helper, who takes us, as it were, by the hand, and leads us to the door, and brings us near the throne, and even puts our petitions into our hearts and mouths, that we may speak acceptable words in the ear of the King. We owe it to our fellow-men, whose wants are many, whose necessities are greater than ours, but who know of no such way of access; who feel that they have no such liberty of petition, who, while we draw near to our Father with filial confidence, stand without in cruel poverty, in hopeless misery, in mute despair, but their imploring eyes and their whole aspect and condition send after us the touching cry, "Pray for us!"

Prayer is a *privilege.* We owe it not only to our fellow-men and our God, but also to ourselves. It is an unspeakable honor and pleasure to draw near to the King of kings with petitions for ourselves; and it is perhaps a greater honor and pleasure to be intrusted and commissioned, so to speak, to present before him the wants and requests of others.

He is so condescending and kind, yet so wise and good, that it fills our whole souls with delight to see his face and hear his voice, and be for a season in his presence. Moreover, we are sure to receive rich gifts and great blessings from him. He has even promised to give us every thing we ask for; or, if we ask for any thing that is not best for us, to give us something better. Indeed, we never get any thing that is really good without asking it of him. We get things in other ways, and from other sources, but they never do us any good.

Prayer is a rich *talent* with which he has intrusted us ; a great power which he has put into our hands,—which he expects us to use to the best possible advantage, and for the improvement of which we must soon give account. We have no more right to neglect this talent, or this power, than we have to neglect our bodily health and strength, or waste our property or time, or bury our talents or influence. Nay, it is our *best* talent, our *greatest* power, our *mightiest* engine of influence ; and not to use it any where, where it might do great good, is to be delinquent in a most important duty, to betray a most sacred trust. Here is an engine of immense moral power. It is God's appointed instrumentality for the salvation of men and the renovation of the world. It has been used in times past by patriarchs and prophets, and apostles and martyrs, and the sacramental host of the Lord's anointed, with the grandest and most beneficent results. Its use now devolves on *us*. In the nature of the case, we alone—the church of God now on the earth—can use it. The world is looking on, waiting, suffering, groaning, dying for its energies to be employed for their redemption. God also looks and waits for us to wield the engine that is to save the world,—to take hold of the power that moves the universe. And now are we at liberty to sit still and do nothing, or to take hold of such a power languidly and apply it just as much, or just as little, as we please ? Can there be any greater guilt than to waste such a talent, to let such a power, under such circumstances, lie useless? When God says to his people, "Ask what I shall give you; demand of me now that great blessing upon the church and the world," can there be a greater insult offered to his infinite majesty than to ask nothing?

Prayer is the great *desideratum of our age.* The church in past ages, in her best ages at least, has been poor in this world's goods, but rich in faith and prayer; weak in worldly power and resources, but mighty in prayer. The church in our day is in danger of reversing the order. She is growing rich in worldly possessions, but poor, we fear, in prayer; strong in human wisdom and might, but weak in faith and the power of God. We have got up some machinery of *our own;* very good so far as it goes, very beautiful in its organization and grand in its proportions, but utterly destitute of any moving power in itself; and yet, alas for human wisdom in its best estate! we are so absorbed and delighted with the goodly mechanism, that we are in danger of forgetting the moving power. We have built the engine and filled it with wood and water, and look on to see it move; but where, alas! is the fire from heaven, that alone can put it in motion! We have stretched the telegraphic wires around the globe; but where is the electric fluid, that can, not only bear the glad tidings of salvation to the ear of the distant heathen, but send it throbbing and thrilling through the inmost fibres of his heart? When, in answer to the united and believing prayers of the whole church, the Spirit of God descends, like a rushing mighty wind, like an irresistible sacred fire from heaven,—

then, and not till then, some good will come of all our voluntary associations and institutions of learning and pecuniary contributions.

Let us not, however, speak uncharitably. There is doubtless much prayer offered by the church in our day, and much good has resulted from our literary and charitable institutions. But how much less than if the breath of life and the Spirit of the living God had been more effectually breathed into them in answer to the effectual fervent prayers of Christians! Let the church be tempted to lay her head in fond dalliance on the lap of worldly wisdom, or wealth or greatness, and in blind forgetfulness or careless neglect of prayer, and she will soon be shorn of her strength and delivered into the hands of her enemies.

2. Special inducements to pray for *colleges.*

Our Lord has commanded it. Among the few special objects of prayer which Jesus enjoined upon his disciples, was the raising up and sending forth of preachers of the gospel. As he lifted up his eyes on the multitudes that flocked to hear him, and saw the field already ripe for the harvest, he turned to his disciples, and said, "The harvest truly is great, and the laborers are few; pray ye, therefore, the Lord of the harvest, that he will send forth laborers into his harvest." Here is our authority. Here, too, is our motive; it is the command of Jesus, who is our master and our friend, and who would fain be the master and friend of all mankind; who has died for our redemption, and died also for theirs; who waits to see the travail of his soul in their conversion, but who cannot see it, humanly speaking,—nay, according to the divine plan and purpose cannot see it, except through the education and commission of an adequate number of suitably qualified ministers of the gospel. And this in our day can be realized only by the blessing of God and the outpouring of his Spirit on our colleges. As we love Christ, then, or the souls for whom Christ died ; as we would honor and obey him ourselves, or see him honored and obeyed by others, we must pray for his blessing on our colleges.

They *need* our *prayers*. The *officers* need them,—they feel that they need them. They are oppressed with the weight of their responsibilities ; not, indeed, all of them,—not any of them perhaps at all times, never any of them probably as they should be,—but some of them, sometimes at least, are oppressed with the weight of their responsibilities, and ready to cry out, "Who is sufficient for these things ?" A crisis comes in the finances of a college, in the government and instruction, in the social habits and moral character of the young men, or in their religious condition and eternal destiny ; when they feel that more than human wisdom, and a greater than human power, is needful to give the right direction to so many young minds, in whom are bound up so many precious interests, and who are destined to exert so wide and so powerful an influence. Then their first recourse is to God in prayer ; and if they could whisper in the ears of Christians every where what they most desire from *them*, it would be, in the words of the apostle, "Brethren, pray for us." Especially on the recurrence of the day set apart by the churches to be observed annually as a day of united prayer for colleges, when the temporal and eternal welfare of so many of their pupils is brought to a crisis,—when the prosperity of the college, the interests of the church and the well-being of the community are so deeply involved,—when all these momentous interests are concentrated, as it were, in a point, and suspended on a few short weeks, when a few days even may turn the scale and decide the question,—then, with unutterable longings, do they wish that all the churches, and all who know how to pray, would pray for colleges.

Next to the rulers of the State and the nation, no class of men have a stronger claim on the prayers of the church than the officers of our colleges. And, in one respect, their claim is prior even to that of civil rulers. The education of civil rulers themselves is, for the most part, intrusted to their hands.

The *students* need our prayers,—peculiarly need them. They are at a peculiarly susceptible and critical age. They are placed in peculiarly trying circumstances. Consciously or unconsciously, they are passing the most important four years of their existence,—deciding questions for themselves which it never will be in their power to decide again; exerting an influence on others, which they will never have the opportunity to exert any where else. Young men are "*strong*;" and now they are to decide the question, whether they shall be strong to do good, or strong to do evil. College life abounds in helps and in hindrances to moral excellence; and now they are to determine, by their own free choice, whether the hindrances shall prevail over the helps, or the helps triumph over the hindrances. The *pious students* need our prayers, that they may be living epistles of Christ, where so many eyes are constantly reading them that will not read the written Word of God ; and that when they go forth into the world, they may go, not mere "*professors* of religion," not ordinary Christians and commonplace ministers, but eminently holy and wise to win souls. The irreligious students need our prayers, that they may escape the many temptations incident to youth and college life ; that they may not make shipwreck of themselves and many others for time and eternity ; that they may not go out into the world educated and accomplished enemies of God and ministers of sin, but may be fitted by converting and sanctifying grace to serve God in their generation.

We should pray for colleges because they *deserve* our prayers. They are not all that they should be—they are not all that they will be. They are constantly rising in the standard of scholarship. They have made no inconsiderable advances in piety in the course of half a century. There is still room for progress in both these respects. Perhaps they may gradually be still more popularized and conformed to the peculiar demands of the country and the age, without sacrificing any of those essential excellencies which have come down from past generations.

But as they have been and are, they have filled their place well, and acted well their part. They have done honor to themselves, and shed lustre on our country,—on the Church and the State, on our politics and history, and literature and religion. The names of their presidents and professors not only shine as a crown of glory on the brow of the colleges, but, like a necklace of pearls, encircle and adorn our common country. What a list of presidents is that which adorns the catalogue of Harvard,—from a Dunster and a Chauncey to an Everett and a Sparks! What a row of presidents lie buried in the graveyard at Princeton! What names in our theological literature, or the theological literature of the world, are brighter than those of Mather and Witherspoon, and Edwards and Davies, and Dwight and Appleton! Posterity will delight to honor not a few of those who now preside over our colleges as scarcely less conspicuous in the history of science and philology. We dare not enter upon the endless task of enumerating the *professors*, and their contributions to classical and polite literature, to ethical and political, physical and metaphysical philosophy. And we can only allude to the alumni of the colleges, who constitute the brightest constellations in our literary and political firmament, —the lights of American history, and the guiding stars which wise men of the Old World have seen in their Eastern homes, and are following Westward to the birthplace of political and religious freedom.

Nor are we less proud or less delighted when we think how many of these honored names are "names written in heaven;" how many of these brilliant constellations in our literary and political heavens will shine as the brightness of the firmament, and as the stars for ever and ever. Be it ours to pray that such stars shall never cease to rise from our colleges, to il-

9*

lumine the churches, and to shed lustre on the country in the sight of men and angels.

We should pray for colleges because they were *founded by the church*, and the church is committed and pledged to sustain them. They were founded in faith and prayer; and they can stand on no other foundation. Money cannot make them prosperous. They may even die of plethora. The State cannot sustain them; they will perish in her cold embrace. They cannot rely on the patronage of the great, or the favor of the people. These would not always stand by them if they could, and could not sustain them even if they would. The church—we have said it repeatedly, but we can hardly say it too often—the church is their mother; and will a mother cast off her daughters without a dowry, or send them away without her prayers? We owe it to the history of American colleges; we owe it, also, to the credit and consistency of the American churches, that no alienation or separation be ever allowed to arise between them.

We owe it especially to those wise and holy men who, from year to year and generation to generation, in weakness and poverty, with much self-denial and many sacrifices, planted these institutions, and watered them with their prayers and tears. Should the churches and their ministers in our day cease to pray for the colleges, we might well believe that the spirits of the many ministers and Christians, who wept and prayed, and toiled over their foundations, could not rest in their heavenly spheres, but would come down to haunt us in our dreams; and we may be sure they will rise up in the judgment and testify against us for our unfaithfulness to the sacred trust which they so solemnly, and at so much expense, bequeathed to us. We seem to see ourselves compassed about by a great cloud of witnesses, who bend from their thrones in heaven, who hover around these seats, sacred to learning and religion, and beseech us to remember them in our supplications. The fathers of Harvard are there with drooping wing and melancholy aspect; and in plaintive tones, they call upon the Christians of Massachusetts and of New England never to cease praying for that apostate, but still beloved college, till it is once more true to its motto—again sacred "to Christ and the church." Those "eleven ministers," and not a few other worthies of the Old Connecticut Colony, are there. Their wing droops not. Joy beams from their eyes, and speaks in the very tones of their voices; but they rejoice with trembling, and warn the officers and pious students, the patrons and friends of the college, all the patrons and friends of learning and religion, not to forget that Yale College was founded in prayer; and prayer alone can sustain it—prayer alone can secure the ends of its establishment.

Time would fail us to enumerate other groups as they pass in long line and regular succession before us,—the founders and early benefactors of Nassau Hall and Dartmouth, and Middlebury and Williams and Amherst. And yet we *must* pause here, and indulge a moment the memory of our hearts, for these are familiar forms and faces. Those ministers and deacons, and private Christians of "Old Hampshire County," how have we seen and heard them pray with strong crying and tears, as they deliberated on the ways and means, and labored on the foundations of a Charity School for the glory of God in the education of Christian ministers and missionaries. And shall its officers and pious students, shall its guardians and patrons and friends in the vicinity and the Commonwealth, shall the friends of education and religion any where, ever forget to pray for Amherst College? If we do, "let our right hand forget its cunning, and our tongue cleave to the roof of our mouth."

Again, the procession passes on. The representatives of still more recent colleges, founded many of them in the New States, come into view. Among them, home missionaries hold a prominent place. Weary and wayworn, poorly clad, but covered with the wounds and scars of their glorious warfare, which adorn them more than imperial purple, they draw near and tell us how, as they laid the foundations of these institutions, they kneeled down on the ground, perchance on the snow, and dedicated them to the service of the living God,—the Father, the Son and the Holy Ghost.

And now, having passed in single file before us, these departed worthies all gather around us again, and hover over us a great cloud of witnesses, and implore us by all that is sacred in their memories, as well all that is precious in the ark of God, always and every where to pray for the colleges.

We should pray for colleges because we owe them a *debt of gratitude*, which can be paid in no other way. It is a dictate of nature that we should pray for our benefactors. And the colleges are the common benefactors—the munificent benefactors, too—of all classes of men in almost every relation, whether of this life only, or also of that which is to come.

They contribute largely to the material wealth of the country; and that not merely in the various economical applications of science, but in the general intelligence, right principles and good influences, which, emanating from these centres, diffuse themselves through society. For knowledge is wealth, good order and good morals are wealth; and a well-educated man, especially if he be also an enlightened Christian, is a mine of wealth in any community.

But we are indebted to them not only for money, —if that were all, the debt might be paid in money. We are indebted to them for great and good men, and, what in our day is second only to such men, for great and good books. Our colleges stand, as it were, behind the press, and directly or indirectly control its issues, which are now so prolific of good or evil. They underlie all our systems of education, government and religion; the foundations on which they rest,—the quarry on, and with which they are built,—the deep fountains from which all these wells and streams are perennially supplied. They furnish our schools with teachers, the churches with ministers, the State and nation with magistrates. As citizens, we are indebted to them, in large measure, for our ablest statesmen,—our Adamses and Jeffersons, and Hamiltons and Madisons, and Jays and Calhouns, and Websters; and, through these, for our Declaration of Independence, our Constitution and our Union; for the establishment and preservation of our peculiar republican and federal institutions. As Christians, we are indebted to them for our ablest divines and preachers; and, through these, for the defence and propagation of a pure Protestant Christianity, and the general prevalence of truth, order and piety in the churches. As the friends of liberty, humanity and progress, we owe to our own colleges and the universities of Europe the ever-glorious Reformation, the English Bible and worship in the vernacular tongue,—the literature and theology of the Puritans,—the rise of Methodism and renewed spirituality in the Protestant churches; and, in one word, the greater part of those politico-religious reforms which have emancipated the human mind from the thraldom of ages. As Christian philanthropists, as those who love the souls of men, we cannot but feel under immense obligations to American colleges for the first impulse and the steady support which they have given to revivals of religion and Christian missions, which have refreshed the parched places of Israel, and watered even the deserts of heathenism; and which already—when their influence has but just begun—have brought such a multitude of souls from every continent and island home to their heavenly Father's house, to go no more out for ever. Oh, how many lights would be put out on earth,—lights in the church, lights in the State and lights in the community,—and how many stars would fall, like Lucifer, from heaven, if merely those who have been *converted* in college, together with those saved through their instrumentality, were blotted from the book of life.

We should pray for colleges because we are *still dependent* on them for the same services; and, if we are instant in prayer, we may hope for yet *richer blessings* from them in time to come. The colleges must continue to be in future, what they always have been, the keystones of our educational system, and the foundation stones of our social, political, and religious institutions. And if these fountains of influence—which, it must be confessed, is still a mixed influence, sending forth not a little that is evil with far more that is good—if they could be wholly purified, and send forth none but streams of truth and righteousness; if all who go forth from them could but go forth, not only with thoroughly disciplined and richly stored minds, but also with renewed and sanctified hearts, full of love to God and man, how would they water all the City of God, and turn the very desert into the garden of the Lord!

We should pray for colleges because they are in *themselves* an exceedingly *interesting subject* of prayer. Look at the students simply as so many young men gathered, we might almost say, *selected* from all parts of the country, the chosen representatives of so many thousand families; young men of superior talents and aspiring aims, full of life and hope, overflowing with sympathy and warm affections; their minds and hearts throbbing and swelling with *new* truths, *new* thoughts and *new* emotions; their whole souls budding and blossoming in youth and beauty, and their characters rapidly forming, in the Spring-time of life, for a harvest of no ordinary glory, or no common shame! With ten thousand such youth before us, so soon to go forth into the world and take possession of its high places of power and influence, may we not well adopt the apostle's reason, and say, "We will pray for you, young men, because ye are *strong?*"

We should pray for colleges because, in so doing, we pray for *every thing else.* In the present members of our colleges, we have the future teachers and rulers of our nation,—the professional men and men of influence of the coming generation,—the rising hope of our country, the church and the world. In praying for them, therefore, we pray for our country in its magistrates, for the church in its ministers, for the world in its missionaries, for every good cause in its future agents and representatives,—for all the streams of influence in their fountain and source. If prayer is the lever that is to raise this fallen world, here, *in our colleges,* is the place to apply it. If prayer is the engine that is to put in motion the whole train of redeeming influences, here is the point to which it should be attached. If prayer is the conductor, which is to convey divine influences from heaven to earth, these are the summits where especially it should be set up, and whence those influences will spread, like the electric fluid, through all the ranks and departments of society.

3. We feel constrained to say a few words, in conclusion, touching the *time* and *manner* of prayer for colleges.

We should at all events pray for them once a year,

at each return of the annual concert of prayer. This the churches have volunteered to do, and this at least the colleges have a right to expect. And oh, if Christians did but know what eventful issues for themselves and their children, for the Commonwealth and the country, for the church and the world, are crowded within the twelve hours of that single day, they would all, with one heart, spend that day in prayer for colleges. And if in so doing they should faint, or fall asleep, would they not hear their Lord saying to them, as to the disciples in Gethsemane, "What! could ye not watch with me one hour?" The whole church with one accord in prayer for that one thing, the conversion of young men in college! with what irresistible power would the very thought stir the inmost soul of the most careless student, and how surely would this natural influence be met and accompanied in the same youthful hearts by a mightier supernatural influence brought down from heaven by the *united* "prayers of the whole church unto God!" Will not ministers, who *do* know the unspeakable interest and importance of this concert, preach on the subject, and endeavor to bring their churches *all* up to its constant and faithful observance?

A *monthly* concert of prayer for this express object would not be more than the object deserves; and but for the fear of multiplying such occasions so as to impair the power and interest of them all, we would make the proposal. We may, at least, be permitted to suggest the inquiry, whether there can be any more proper subject for at least *one* prayer in each of the monthly concerts that are now observed, than those literary institutions, which alone can furnish *suitable men* to take the lead in every enterprise of benevolence and reform ?

Are not colleges entitled, also, to a distinct remembrance in the public worship of the sanctuary ? Should the minister of the gospel, Sabbath after Sabbath, pass without a word of recognition the very institutions in which he himself, and nearly all who, like him, minister at the altar in other churches, gained their preparation of mind—perchance of *heart* also—to lead in the devotions of the sanctuary ? Is it not the duty of ministers thus publicly to attest before the people their convictions of the intimate connection between the colleges and the interests of the church, and thus, by example, teach them to pray for literary institutions ? Aside from the direct efficacy of such public prayers, they would tend indirectly to remove popular prejudice, to strengthen the confidence and deepen the interest of common minds in colleges, and to induce a larger number of young men of suitable talents to seek an education for the gospel ministry.

May we not also ask for the colleges an interest in the prayers of intelligent and pious families at the family altar ? Those parents who have sons in college cannot but remember them and, we trust, their fellow-students also, with the tenderest solicitude, every morning and evening. Others cannot feel their personal interest ; but, if they obey the golden rule, or if they pray for objects according to their intrinsic merits or their relative importance, will they not often pray, in the family and in the closet, for the outpouring of the Spirit on the thousands of young men in our colleges ?

We should pray for colleges *now*,—in this eventful age of the world, when God is overturning obstacles and opening all nations to the spread of the gospel ; when Europe is crying in piteous tones for help, and Ethiopia is stretching forth her hands unto the Lord ; and even China is waking from her sleep of ages, and feeling after the true God, if haply she might find him ;—in this interesting crisis of our country's destiny, when vast hordes of Celtic papists and Teutonic infidels are invading it on the East, and pagans from China are beginning to land on our Western coast ; and the question is not whether we can conquer them in battle, but whether we can take them in with our population, and assimilate them to our own political and religious institutions ; and when the still more momentous question is to be decided (decided, too, by our public, and, for the most part, by our *educated* men), whether this boasted land of liberty shall take the lead, by precept and example, in " breaking every yoke," or shall become the most unblushing and the most powerful propagandist of slavery on the face of the earth ;—in the new and strange position of the missionary enterprise, when the home and the foreign fields have met on our own shores, and it is all white for the harvest, but when neither the Home nor the Foreign Missionary Society can find the laborers they want for the *cultivation* of any part of it ;—in the present state of the churches and the colleges, when after having advanced for years in the frequency of revivals and the number of conversions, they have commenced a retrograde movement, whereby there is a constant decrease of the ministers just when there is the most urgent demand for a great and constant increase. At such a crisis, with what weight and power does the command of our Saviour fall upon our ears: "The harvest truly is great, and the laborers are few; pray ye, therefore, the Lord of the harvest, that he will send forth laborers into his harvest."

And now as to the manner of prayer, we should endeavor to pray with all the characteristics of prevailing prayer,—"the effectual fervent prayer of the righteous man, which availeth much."

First of all, we must have a sincere desire for the blessing which we ask; for to ask for that blessing while we do not really desire it, is a mockery and insult. Moreover, our desires should be intelligent and fervent, springing from and proportioned to a just appreciation of the transcendent importance of the object.

We should be importunate and persevering in our supplications. We should not merely ask but seek, not merely seek but knock, till the door of heavenly mercy is thrown open before us. We expect by importunity and perseverance to prevail with our friends and neighbors, with strangers, with our fellow-men generally, even with those that "fear not God, nor regard men." And "will not God hear his own elect who cry day and night unto him, though he bear long with them? I tell you he will hear them speedily."

We must pray expecting to receive the blessing for

which we pray; for without faith, it is impossible to please him; and in this matter, as in every thing else for which we pray and labor, it will be just according to our faith. In some things that we ask for ourselves for the present life, we may well be in doubt, for we do not know whether they are for our good, or agreeable to his will; but in asking for spiritual blessings for ourselves or others, there is no room for doubt. In regard to colleges especially, God has already revealed his will, and shown most unequivocally his willingness to bless them in answer to the prayers of his people. "And if we ask any thing according to his will, he heareth us. And if we know that he heareth us, whatsoever we ask, we know that we have the petitions that we desired of him."

But this faith must be accompanied with deep humility, like that of the centurion, who, though clothed with authority by the Romans, and pronounced worthy by the elders of the Jews, did not deem himself worthy that Jesus of Nazareth should come under his roof; like that of Abraham, who, while he intercedes for Sodom like an angel, or a friend of the Most High, acknowledges that he is but dust and ashes; like that of Jacob, who, in one breath, says, "I will not let thee go except thou bless me;" and in another adds, "I am not worthy of the least of all thy mercies."

Humility and penitence naturally lead to fasting, and fasting adds not a little to the efficacy of prayer. If we would cast out the evil spirit from our colleges, that the Holy Spirit may enter in and dwell there, we must not forget that "this kind goeth not forth but by prayer and fasting."

Finally, the ultimate aim and end of all our prayers should be not that we may be gratified, or even that the common interests of learning and religion may be advanced, but that "God in all things may be glorified through Jesus Christ." Who that loves the Saviour, and longs to have him "see of the travail of his soul and be satisfied," would not delight, above all things, to see him honored by the cordial love and service of all the young men in our colleges; and who that has the spirit of those holy men of old, who spake as they were moved by the Holy Ghost, will not unite in the prayers which patriarchs and prophets have so often and so effectually offered: "What wilt thou do unto *thy great name.* Do thou it for *thy name's* sake. O Lord, hear; O Lord, forgive; O Lord, hearken and do: defer not, for thy *city* and thy *people* are *called* by *thy name.*"

THE END.

www.ingramcontent.com/pod-product-compliance
Lightning Source LLC
LaVergne TN
LVHW011207110826
845150LV00006B/1354

* 9 7 8 1 4 2 5 5 1 8 0 0 4 *